CONTENTS

INTRODUCTION

Earlier editions of *Missouri: Then and Now* introduced a generation of students to the story of their state and its people. This new and enlarged edition promises to equip young Missourians for the challenges of the twenty-first century. Closely correlated with Missouri's Show-Me Standards, it contains useful features that have been carefully constructed to facilitate student mastery of the basic competencies measured by the Missouri Assessment Program.

The text incorporates geography, civics, economics, anthropology, and sociology with history to give students an opportunity to learn about the world on several levels: the community (the origin and subsequent growth of towns), the region (the occupation and settlement of the Mississippi River valley and the Louisiana Purchase), the nation (the struggle for statehood and the debate over slavery, the western movement, the Civil War, the Great Depression of the 1930s, and the Civil Rights movement) and the world (exploration, world wars, the global economy, and the worldwide communications network). This new edition also incorporates valuable new insights concerning the importance of scientific and technological innovations.

This combination of the historical, civic-political, social-cultural, economic, and geographic perspectives promises to afford students a clearer understanding of their state, nation, and world. The book also has been designed to foster better understanding among peoples of differing cultural backgrounds by detailing the unique contributions that diverse racial and ethnic groups have made to state and national development.

Missouri: Then and Now is the only fourth-grade Missouri history textbook whose authors are native Missourians and recognized authorities in Missouri studies. In contrast with generic texts that simply plug in occasional stories about Missouri figures, this book offers students a more thoughtful perspective on what it means to be a Missourian. By drawing upon the stories of lesser-known Missouri people and places, the authors are able to bring history home to the students and better capture the essence of the state.

Missouri: Then and Now has been written with both students and teachers in mind. This latest edition combines the attributes that made previous editions a highly usable and practical text with important new features that will further enhance its value as an instructional tool.

* The story-like text will appeal to fourth graders, and the vocabulary and sentence construction are appropriate for their grade level.

* Both the text and the student learning activities have been carefully coordinated with Missouri's Show-Me knowledge and performance standards.

* For each chapter this *Teacher's Guide* provides suggested Guiding Questions with the applicable Missouri knowledge standards identified for each individual question. Teachers also will find a wide array of carefully constructed sample

Learning Activities designed to address state performance standards. The applicable standards are referenced for each activity.

* The text is profusely illustrated with more than 170 photographs, maps, time lines, and drawings, many of them in color.

* Famous Missourians sections feature individuals who have made special contributions to the state.

* In Their Own Words sections allow students to read excerpts from letters, diaries, reports, and other historical documents.

* Each chapter begins with Guiding Questions intended to help students formulate their own ideas and initiate individual and group research activities.

* A listing of recent books, videos, and web sites at the end of each chapter will lead students to information sources related to Missouri topics.

* The new words identified for each chapter and the glossary placed in the appendix provide useful tools for vocabulary building.

* Stories about the experiences of lesser-known Missourians provide a personal touch and afford students a better understanding of how significant historical events can affect ordinary people.

* Students will recognize many cities, towns, and other Missouri places mentioned in the text.

* Dates have been deemphasized in favor of time lines located throughout the book to give students a sense of chronology.

* This *Teacher's Guide* also includes a summary of principal points covered in the text for each chapter and a brief bibliography of general reference works.

A Special Note to Teachers and Curriculum Designers

The opportunities and the demands posed by Missouri's Show-Me Standards and the Missouri Assessment Program present classroom teachers with daunting challenges. *Missouri: Then and Now* and this accompanying *Teacher's Guide* have been designed to assist teachers and curriculum designers, who experience so many demands on their time, with the application of the Show-Me Standards to a Missouri history curriculum for fourth graders.

It is impossible to cover everything, but with the individual guidelines for each chapter that are included in this Guide, you will be able to select both topics and activities that will interest your students and also address Missouri's Show-Me Standards. These instructional aids will allow you and your colleagues to fashion a curriculum plan suitable for your particular school, and at the same time ensure that you are equipping your students with the factual knowledge and basic skills they will need to be successful. Because the applicable knowledge and performance standards have been carefully identified, you will find it possible to build lesson plans suited to the topics that you have chosen to emphasize. The numerous learning activities found in the text and in this Guide have been designed to offer the kinds of active learning experiences that will enable students to master the competencies measured by the Missouri Assessment Program. The authors welcome teacher reactions and suggestions that could be used to improve future editions.

THE SHOW-ME STANDARDS: SOCIAL STUDIES

In Social Studies, students in Missouri public schools will acquire a solid foundation that includes knowledge of:

1. principles expressed in the documents shaping constitutional democracy in the United States.

2. continuity and change in the history of Missouri, the United States, and the world.

3. principles and processes of governance systems.

4. economic concepts (including productivity and the market system) and principles (including the law of supply and demand).

5. the major elements of geographical study and analysis (such as location, place, movement, regions) and their relationship to changes in society and environment.

6. relationships of the individual and groups to institutions and cultural traditions.

7. the use of tools of social science inquiry, such as surveys, statistics, maps, and documents.

CHAPTER 1
THE FIRST MISSOURIANS

What All Students Should Know

The Guiding Questions listed below are correlated with the text and intended to assist teachers and curriculum designers with the development of unit and lesson plans. The applicable Show-Me Knowledge Standards for Social Studies are referenced in parentheses at the end of each question. A listing of those standards can be found on page 5 of this Guide.

1. How do we learn about people who lived before there were written records? What are artifacts? How do archaeologists use them to uncover important information about Missouri's earliest inhabitants? (SS7)

2. Why is it useful to know in what order things occurred? What is a time line and how do you construct one? (SS2; SS7)

3. How do environmental changes alter the way people live? What were some of the changes that occurred when the earth got warmer at the end of the Ice Age? How did the melting of the glaciers affect the land bridge that once connected North America and Asia? Why do scientists think the warm climate may have contributed to the disappearance of some prehistoric animals? (SS5)

4. How did different groups of Indian people who once lived in Missouri build their houses, get their food, obtain their clothing, and make their tools? (SS5; SS6; SS7)

5. How were Indians who lived in other parts of North America different from those who lived in early Missouri? (SS5; SS6; SS7)

6. How was Indian life changed after the European settlers came to Missouri? (SS2; SS4; SS6; SS7)

7. What kinds of things did the European settlers learn from their Indian neighbors? (SS2; SS6)

8. How and why did Indians and European settlers in Missouri have different ideas about how to live and to make the best use of the region where they lived? (SS5; SS6; SS7)

What All Students Should Be Able to Do

1.1. Develop questions and ideas to initiate and refine research.

1.2. Conduct research to answer questions and evaluate information and ideas.

1.3. Design and conduct field and laboratory investigations to study nature and society.

1.4. Use technological tools and other resources to locate, select, and organize information.

1.5. Comprehend and evaluate written, visual, and oral presentations and works.

1.6. Discover and evaluate patterns and relationships in information.

1.7. Evaluate the accuracy of information and ideas and the reliability of their sources.

1.8. Organize data, information, and ideas into useful forms for analysis or presentation.

1.9. Identify, analyze, and compare the institutions, traditions, and art forms of past and present societies.

1.10. Apply acquired information, ideas, and skills to different contexts.

2.1. Plan and make written, oral, and visual presentations for a variety of purposes and audiences.

2.2. Review and revise communications to improve accuracy and clarity.

2.3. Exchange information, questions, and ideas while recognizing the perspectives of others.

2.4. Present perceptions and ideas regarding works of the arts, humanities, and sciences.

2.5. Perform or produce works in the fine and practical arts.

2.7. Use technological tools to exchange information and ideas.

3.1. Identify problems and define their scope and elements.

3.2. Develop and apply strategies based on ways others have prevented or solved problems.

3.3. Develop and apply strategies based on one's own experiences in preventing or solving problems.

3.4. Evaluate the processes used in recognizing and solving problems.

3.5. Reason inductively from a set of specific facts and deductively from general premises.

3.6. Examine problems and proposed solutions from multiple perspectives.

3.7. Evaluate the extent to which a strategy addresses the problem.

3.8. Assess costs, benefits, and other consequences of proposed solutions.

4.1. Explain reasoning and identify information used to support decisions.

4.2. Understand and apply the rights and responsibilities of citizenship in Missouri and in the United States.

4.3. Analyze the duties and responsibilities of individuals in societies.

4.4. Recognize and practice honesty and integrity in academic work.

4.5. Develop, monitor, and revise plans of action to meet deadlines and accomplish those tasks.

Sample Learning Activities

The applicable Show-Me Performance Standards are referenced in parentheses.

* Invite students to generate a list of questions about Missouri's Indian inhabitants that interest them. Assist them in refining those questions and use them to guide their research—the suggested Guiding Questions should help facilitate this process. This process would be a good way to introduce each new chapter. (1.1)

* Use a globe to point out the location of the Bering Sea. Explain to the students that it was once a land bridge that connected North America and Asia until the melting glaciers caused ocean levels to rise and flood low-lying areas such as this. (1.5)

* Have a discussion about the difference between archaeology and history. Archaeologists use artifacts and historians work mostly from written records--letters, diaries, journals, newspapers, and legal documents. This might also be a good time to explore the differences between written and oral sources. This will set the stage for future discussions about how to read and evaluate written sources. The documents featured in most chapters will provide opportunities to explore many of these issues. (1.7)

* Explain the time line on page xii to the students. Help students understand the importance of cause-effect relationships. Dates and chronology are difficult concepts for children to understand. To communicate clearly when past events took place, it is helpful to use terms such as minutes, hours, days, or years ago, expressions such as long ago or when our parents were my age, or dates such as 1776 and 2001. You might find it helpful to obtain a long wire to use as a chronology indicator and hang it between the walls of your classroom. Attach cards with events written on them onto the wire in the order that they happened. Refer the class to the time "line" throughout your study of Missouri. You may want to remove all but a few important cards on the wire and attach new ones as you proceed through the text. (1.6)

* Have each student make a time line for her or his own life. (1.10)

* Use the questions that the students formulated to help them make some generalizations about how Indian people lived in different times and places. Be sure to explain that all Indian people were not the same; they lived in very different ways and spoke different languages. Remind the students to use modifiers, such as usually, most, and some, when making general statements. Ask the students to consider how the physical characteristics (plants, animals, terrain, weather, etc.) of a region might have affected the way Indian people lived. Have them collect infor-

mation about some of the differences among the lifestyles of Indians who lived in well-watered, wooded areas with those who resided in dry, treeless regions. Guide the students in drawing some conclusions about their generalizations. Among other things you can ask them to compare how Indian people built their houses, got their food, obtained their clothing, and made their tools. The Think/Pair/Share approach is an excellent cooperative learning structure that helps students form generalizations and draw conclusions. (1.1; 1.2; 1.6; 2.1; 2.3)

* Have each pupil write a paragraph summarizing the conclusions reached in class discussions. Possible topics include "Indian People Had to Know Many Things" or "Native Americans Used Things around Them." (1.5; 2.1)

* Arrange for your class to visit a prehistoric archaeological site or a museum containing Native American artifacts. If that is not feasible, invite someone familiar with Native American life and customs to talk to your class and perhaps show them some interesting Indian artifacts. (1.3)

* Divide the class into groups and assign each group to log on to one of the web sites listed at the end of the chapter. Help them summarize their findings and ask them to share that information with the rest of the class. (1.2; 1.4; 2.1)

* Have the students read George Sibley's version of Big Soldier's thoughts about white settlement on pages 18-19 of the text. Ask them to consider how Big Soldier's views would have differed from those of white settlers in Missouri. The white settlers favored a more sedentary existence with their houses and fields enclosed by fences. Because they settled down in one place, they used equipment and tools that would have been difficult for the Indians to transport as they moved about. The Indians preferred a more nomadic way of life that took them various places in search of wild game. After they planted their fields, they went off on hunting expeditions and returned later to harvest their crops. (1.5; 3.6)

* Let each student write a short paper on how the contributions of early Indian people in Missouri affect our lives today. (1.9; 2.1)

SUMMARY OF PRINCIPAL POINTS

Missouri's first people were the Native Americans. They lived in the area for at least ten thousand years before the Europeans arrived. This chapter traces some of the major Native American groups throughout those years and describes how they lived. The Europeans called the Native Americans "Indians." The book and this Guide use both terms interchangeably. The chapter concludes by showing how the arrival of the Europeans affected the Indian way of life. It also shows how the Native Americans influenced the life of the new settlers who came to

Missouri. The Osage Indian leader Big Soldier is the subject of the Famous Missourian sketch and also is featured in the In Their Own Words section.

ANSWERS TO QUESTIONS AND EXERCISES IN THE TEXT

In Their Own Words

1. Answers will vary. Suggested: their fields, gardens, farm animals, machines, and clothing. He also believed that they did not have as much freedom to move about as Indian people. The Americans seemed more tied to one place.

2. Answers may vary. Suggested: He had seen them make clothes from cotton and flax using spinning wheels and looms. The Indians made their clothes from animal skins and furs.

3. They believed that the Indians should settle down and live, work, and dress like them. They considered their own ways better than Indian ways. They thought that the Indians were wild and ignorant and could not understand why they did not want to change.

4. He was free to move about. He did not have to stay in the same place and work in the fields all day. He could hunt and roam.

5. George Sibley wrote down what he heard Big Soldier say, but many years had passed since they had talked and people sometimes forget things. Even though Sibley admired Big Soldier, he still found it difficult to understand the Indian viewpoint. He even said that Big Soldier was ignorant and too old to change. Big Soldier could have better explained the reasons that he felt the way he did.

Matching Partners

1-c; 2-b; 3-d; 4-a

Testing Yourself

1. Scientists think the first Indians came across a land bridge that once connected Asia with North America. They were searching for game animals and probably did not know that they had entered a new continent.

2. Mammoth, mastodon, and prehistoric bison.

3. The Missouri weather caused the wooden and clay buildings to decay rapidly once the Indians had left.

4. Osage, Missouri, Shawnee, Delaware, Peorias, Kickapoo, Sac, Fox, Kansas, and Ioway.

5. Osage men were the hunters and warriors. The women prepared the animals killed by the men, farmed, made most of the tools in the home, built the lodges, prepared the food, took care of the children, and carried the supplies.

6. We have Indian words such as tomahawk, wigwam, and papoose. Indian foods included succotash and hominy. Pumpkins, corn, tomatoes, beans, and

squash were Indian crops. We wear Indian-style clothing such as moccasins, buckskin shirts with fringe, and parkas. We still use the beautiful Indian designs as decorations. The word "Missouri" was an Indian name. Kansas City, Osceola, and Neosho are a few of the Missouri places that have Indian names.

Things to Talk About

1. No. Archaeologists have found artifacts such as tools and implements, arrowheads and spear points, clothes, food, and other items used by the early people.

2. Since they left no written records and no stories have been passed down from that long ago, we have no way of knowing what they called themselves.

3. If any printed words, photographs, or electronic records still exist, they will be able to learn much from them. They will also examine our buildings, furniture, tools, artwork, and other artifacts that should tell much about the way we lived.

4. Answers will vary.

5. The only tame animal the Osage Indian people knew about was the dog. The Plains Indians sometimes used dogs to pull a travois for carrying things.

6. They lived in different locations, so that they were in areas that were good for raising crops during growing and harvesting seasons, and areas where game was plentiful during hunting seasons.

7. Today people often live eighty years or more, but they seldom live more than one hundred years. Many years ago a person's life was much shorter. One person could not live from Columbus's day to the present.

CHAPTER 2
A RICH LAND

What All Students Should Know

The Guiding Questions listed below are correlated with the text and intended to assist teachers and curriculum designers with the development of unit and lesson plans. The applicable Show-Me Knowledge Standards for Social Studies are referenced in parentheses at the end of each question. A listing of those standards can be found on page 5 of this Guide.

1. What natural resources have attracted settlers to Missouri from the earliest times? (SS2; SS5; SS6)

2. How and why did Missouri's geographic location affect its growth and development? Ask students to identify specific geographic features

that were important to Missouri's growth and development. (SS2; SS5; SS6; SS7)

3. What are political boundaries? Why are they important? How do geographic features affect their location? Ask students to identify different kinds of political units that are marked by boundaries (nations, states, and counties in which cities are also found). (SS5; SS6; SS7)

4. What are Missouri's four geographic regions? What kinds of features are used to describe a region? What are distinguishing features for each of Missouri's four geographic regions? (SS5; SS6; SS7)

5. How have geographic features affected settlement and communications in Missouri? (SS2; SS5; SS6)

6. How do a region's flora, fauna, terrain, and weather affect the way people live? How did those physical characteristics shape the lives of Native Americans? (SS5; SS6; SS7)

What All Students Should Be Able to Do

1.1. Develop questions and ideas to initiate and refine research.

1.2. Conduct research to answer questions and evaluate information and ideas.

1.3. Design and conduct field and laboratory investigations to study nature and society.

1.4. Use technological tools and other resources to locate, select, and organize information.

1.5. Comprehend and evaluate written, visual, and oral presentations and works.

1.6. Discover and evaluate patterns and relationships in information.

1.7. Evaluate the accuracy of information and ideas and the reliability of their sources.

1.8. Organize data, information, and ideas into useful forms for analysis or presentation.

1.9. Identify, analyze, and compare the institutions, traditions, and art forms of past and present societies.

1.10. Apply acquired information, ideas, and skills to different contexts.

2.1. Plan and make written, oral, and visual presentations for a variety of purposes and audiences.

2.2. Review and revise communications to improve accuracy and clarity.

2.3. Exchange information, questions, and ideas while recognizing the perspectives of others.

2.4. Present perceptions and ideas regarding works of the arts, humanities, and sciences.

2.5. Perform or produce works in the fine and practical arts.

2.7. Use technological tools to exchange information and ideas.

3.1. Identify problems and define their scope and elements.

3.2. Develop and apply strategies based on ways others have prevented or solved problems.

3.3. Develop and apply strategies based on one's own experiences in preventing or solving problems.

3.4. Evaluate the processes used in recognizing and solving problems.

3.5. Reason inductively from a set of specific facts and deductively from general premises.

3.6. Examine problems and proposed solutions from multiple perspectives.

3.7. Evaluate the extent to which a strategy addresses the problem.

3.8. Assess costs, benefits, and other consequences of proposed solutions.

4.1. Explain reasoning and identify information used to support decisions.

4.2. Understand and apply the rights and responsibilities of citizenship in Missouri and in the United States.

4.3. Analyze the duties and responsibilities of individuals in societies.

4.4. Recognize and practice honesty and integrity in academic work.

4.5. Develop, monitor, and revise plans of action to meet deadlines and accomplish those tasks.

Sample Learning Activities

The applicable Show-Me Performance Standards are referenced in parentheses.

* Invite the students to generate a list of questions about geography, maps, and Missouri places that interest them. Assist them in refining their questions and use them to guide their research—the Guiding Questions should help facilitate the process. (1.1)

* Have the students conduct research to discover how a region's plants, animals, terrain, and weather can affect the way people live and work. The Missouri Botanical Garden's interactive web site www.mobot.org is excellent for this purpose. Click on the section titled Just for Kids. The Biomes of the World section will introduce students to deserts, temperate regions, grasslands, rain forests, etc. Another section, Fresh Water Ecosystems, will enable them to explore such topics as how streams become rivers. (1.1; 1.2; 1.4)

* Create a geography center that contains various geographic tools—globes, atlases, and different types of maps. Discuss with the students the kinds of information each provides and explain how to use them. (1.4)

* A good way to introduce map reading to the students is to have

14

them make a map themselves. Take the class on a tour of the school grounds and neighborhood surrounding the school. Have the students draw a diagram of what they have seen. Go over the cardinal directions and have the students place these on a map. (1.2; 1.6; 1.8)

* Give each student an outline map of the United States. Have them label the Mississippi and the Missouri Rivers. Ask them to identify places where geographic features have determined the location of boundaries in Missouri and in other states. Ask them to speculate about how Missouri's central location and North America's two longest rivers coming together in Missouri might have affected the state's growth and development. Also have them label each of the states that border Missouri. (1.4; 1.6; 2.3)

* Divide the class into four groups. Assign one of Missouri's geographic regions to each group. Each group should then decide what are the most important characteristics of that region (topographical features, natural resources, important products, etc.). Assist them in identifying different sources of information that they can use (the textbook; reference books; web sites, and published materials available from various state agencies—Missouri Departments and Divisions of Tourism; State Parks; Agriculture; Conservation, etc.). Have each group write letters to organizations or state agencies that provide free promotional materials about the region and its attractions. You can call upon the regional groups to provide information related to their region as you study different topics related to Missouri places and people. (1.1; 1.2; 1.4; 1.5; 1.6; 1.8; 2.1; 2.3)

* Have each group make a large chart showing the information they have gathered. They might also make a scrapbook with pictures and other materials that they have collected from various sources. (1.8; 2.1)

* Ask the students to make up questions to ask other members of the class, such as "I have the most cities in the state. Which region am I?" (1.6; 2.3)

* Give each student an outline map of the state. Have each pupil label the geographic regions and place the major towns correctly. Ask them to provide possible explanations for the locations of Jefferson City, St. Louis, and Kansas City and other important cities. (1.6; 1.8)

* Have students frame questions about the history of their city or town that interest them. Collect information about its founders, the date of its founding, who it was named for, how and why its location was selected, and how it has changed since its establishment. Arrange to visit a local historical society library or museum to do research. Use this occasion to show them examples of primary sources. Have someone from the historical society talk about local history. Leave time for the students to ask

15

questions. Have the students plan how to best present the results of their research. They might compile a book containing stories and pictures about the history of their town or community, or they could draw a mural showing important events in their town's history. (1.1; 1.2; 1.3; 2.1; 2.5)

* Make the students aware that every community has historic buildings and places. Ask them to identify historic buildings or places in their community. Assign them to investigate if any places in their county are listed on the National Register of Historic Places. This can be done easily by checking the Missouri National Register of Historic Places List on the internet at www.mostateparks.com/hpp/MNRList.shtm. (Note: The address for this web site has changed since it was printed in the textbook.) If there are no National Register listings for your county, have the students identify such a site in a neighboring county. If possible, arrange for the students to visit one or more National Register properties. They could ask the owners of those sites questions about their property. (1.3; 1.4)

* Assist the students in accessing the Missouri Census Data Center web site, http://mcdc.missouri.edu. Have them look up the population of the state, their county, and their town or city. Ask them to compare the 2000 population figures with the 1990 figures. Assign them to calculate how much the population increased or decreased between 1990 and 2000. Discuss some possible reasons that their area is either growing or not growing. Have the students make a bar graph showing the 1990 and 2000 population figures for the state, county, and city. (1.4; 1.8)

* Have the students conduct research to find out how the construction of dams on Missouri's rivers affected people and places. Ask them to make a chart listing in separate columns the positive and negative consequences of building dams. Then have them decide whether they believe the positive benefits of dams outweigh the negative effects they may cause. (1.2; 1.6; 1.8; 3.1; 3.6; 3.8)

* Gather news clippings that describe the social and political effects of environmental changes resulting from natural disasters (floods, storms, droughts, earthquakes). Have them make a list of ways that governments and communities can address the problems caused by these disasters. (1.2; 1.5; 3.4)

* Have the students make a salt-and-flour topographical map of Missouri (1.2; 1.8). The recipe for modeling material is as follows:
Use twice as much salt as flour.
Heat in a skillet stirring constantly.
When hot, add enough water to form an easily handled dough.
A few drops of food coloring will make the dough more attractive.

SUMMARY OF PRINCIPAL POINTS

This chapter emphasizes several important geography-related competencies. Natural features (continents, oceans, seas, gulfs, lakes, and rivers) and political units (nations, states, and cities) are identified. Students will learn about globes and maps and how to use them to locate regions and places related to Missouri. The four geographical areas in the state are discussed. Students will discover that Missouri's varied and productive soils and its abundance of other natural resources including minerals, timber, water, and wildlife caused many different people to settle in Missouri. The state's location at the heart of the nation's central river system, in addition to the many rivers within its boundaries, made it accessible to early settlers. The rivers connected the state with other parts of North America and the world. The chapter concludes with a discussion of climate and how it influences the way people live.

ANSWERS TO QUESTIONS AND EXERCISES IN THE TEXT

Testing Yourself
1. North America, South America, Africa, Europe, Asia, Australia, and Antarctica.
2. North America.
3. Canada.
4. Mexico.
5. Iowa, Arkansas, Illinois, Kentucky, Tennessee, Nebraska, Kansas, Oklahoma.
6. Missouri River, Mississippi River.
7. Taum Sauk Mountains.
8. Lake of the Ozarks.
9. Cool temperate.

Matching Partners
1-b, 2-c, 3-d, 4-a

Things to Talk About
1. Missouri's central location makes it easy to reach from almost all parts of the country. Missouri's river and transportation systems connect the state with other parts of the United States and the world. The two largest rivers in North America join together in Missouri. Missouri is a crossroads state where the different sections of the country come together.
2. The four cardinal directions are north, south, east, and west. Using a compass offers the easiest way to locate the cardinal directions. If you do not have a compass, there is a simple way to locate the directions. The sun always rises in the east and sets in the west. If you stand with your right arm toward the direction where the sun rises and your left arm toward the direction where it sets, you will

be facing north and your back will be toward the south. Many maps will show the four directions. If not, north is traditionally toward the top of the map. This means that south is toward the bottom, east toward the right-hand side, and west toward the left-hand side.

3. Discussion will vary.

4. Fishing, boating, swimming, waterskiing, and producing electricity.

5. The construction of Bagnell Dam created Missouri's largest lake. When the Lake of the Ozarks was first formed the water covered land where people had lived and worked. They had to leave their homes. Life in the region was very different once the lake was there. It brought many new people into the area. They built new homes and businesses near the lake. The lake became a major recreational area for Missourians. The generators in the dam provided electricity for people in other parts of the state.

6. Swampland does not make good farmland. The canals drained away the water and turned the swamps into good farmland. The trees that grew in the swamps had to be cut down so the area could be cultivated. The loss of the wetlands drove away many wild birds and animals that had lived in the swamplands.

7. Answers will vary.

8. Discussion will vary.

9. The kinds of food, clothing, and shelter would be different. The ways that most people earned their living would also vary.

CHAPTER 3
EUROPE DISCOVERS AMERICA AND MISSOURI

What All Students Should Know

The Guiding Questions listed below are correlated with the text and intended to assist teachers and curriculum designers with the development of unit and lesson plans. The applicable Show-Me Knowledge Standards for Social Studies are referenced in parentheses at the end of each question. A listing of those standards can be found on page 5 of this Guide.

1. Why were Missouri's early settlements located along rivers? (SS2; SS5)

2. Who were some early explorers that played important roles in bringing European settlement to America? What were they seeking? Which of these early explorers do you believe were most important to Missouri? Why? (SS2; SS5; SS6)

3. How and why did explorers from different countries compete to control the region that is today Missouri? (SS2; SS3; SS5; SS7)

4. Why did some early Missouri settlements fail? (SS2; SS4; SS5)

5. How did Missouri change after the Europeans came? (SS2; SS3; SS5; SS6)

What All Students Should Be Able to Do

1.1. Develop questions and ideas to initiate and refine research.

1.2. Conduct research to answer questions and evaluate information and ideas.

1.3. Design and conduct field and laboratory investigations to study nature and society.

1.4. Use technological tools and other resources to locate, select, and organize information.

1.5. Comprehend and evaluate written, visual, and oral presentations and works.

1.6. Discover and evaluate patterns and relationships in information.

1.7. Evaluate the accuracy of information and ideas and the reliability of their sources.

1.8. Organize data, information, and ideas into useful forms for analysis or presentation.

1.9. Identify, analyze, and compare the institutions, traditions, and art forms of past and present societies.

1.10. Apply acquired information, ideas, and skills to different contexts.

2.1. Plan and make written, oral, and visual presentations for a variety of purposes and audiences.

2.2. Review and revise communications to improve accuracy and clarity.

2.3. Exchange information, questions, and ideas while recognizing the perspectives of others.

2.4. Present perceptions and ideas regarding works of the arts, humanities, and sciences.

2.5. Perform or produce works in the fine and practical arts.

2.7. Use technological tools to exchange information and ideas.

3.1. Identify problems and define their scope and elements.

3.2. Develop and apply strategies based on ways others have prevented or solved problems.

3.3. Develop and apply strategies based on one's own experiences in preventing or solving problems.

3.4. Evaluate the processes used in recognizing and solving problems.

3.5. Reason inductively from a set of specific facts and deductively from general premises.

3.6. Examine problems and proposed solutions from multiple perspectives.

3.7. Evaluate the extent to which a strategy addresses the problem.

3.8. Assess costs, benefits, and other consequences of proposed solutions.

4.1. Explain reasoning and identify information used to support decisions.

4.2. Understand and apply the rights and responsibilities of citizenship in Missouri and in the United States.

4.3. Analyze the duties and responsibilities of individuals in societies.

4.4. Recognize and practice honesty and integrity in academic work.

4.5. Develop, monitor, and revise plans of action to meet deadlines and accomplish those tasks.

Sample Learning Activities

The applicable Show-Me Performance Standards are referenced in parentheses.

* Invite the students to generate a list of questions about explorers and exploration that interest them. Assist them in refining those questions and use them to guide their research and study—the Guiding Questions should help facilitate this process. (1.1)

* Review the cardinal directions. Ask a student to locate Europe, Asia, China, India, and Spain on a globe. Ask the class what direction Europe is from the United States. (1.4; 1.6)

* With the class trace the routes taken by Columbus, de Soto, Marquette and Jolliet, and La Salle. (1.5)

* Have students conduct research about early European explorers. Make a chart showing the name of the explorer, the country they came from, and one or two interesting facts about them or their discoveries. (1.2; 1.5; 1.8)

* Using the Think/Pair/Share cooperative learning structure, invite students to identify what kinds of individuals they think would make the best explorers. Ask them to consider what skills and other qualities they think good explorers need. Have them select the explorer that they think was the most successful and tell why. (1.1; 1.2; 1.5; 2.3)

* Dramatize the first meeting between Christopher Columbus and the Indians. (1.2; 2.1; 2.5)

* Invite the students to speculate about what the Native Americans might have thought about people with different-colored skin wearing strange clothes, who had horses, guns, and other strange tools, and who could read from books. Ask them to write a short paragraph telling what things an Indian might have found most interesting or unusual about the strangers who had come to their lands. (1.1; 1.2; 1.9; 2.1; 3.6)

* Ask the students to draw a picture showing something that Father Marquette and Jolliet might have noticed on their expedition down the Mississippi. (1.5; 2.1; 2.5)

* Have students discuss possible reasons that Fort Orleans failed as a settlement and Ste. Genevieve and St. Louis were successful. (1.1; 1.2; 1.6)

* Ask the students to write a letter that they think young Auguste Chouteau might have written to his mother in New Orleans, telling her about his trip up the Mississippi River and the founding of St. Louis. (1.2; 1.5; 2.1)

* Have the students look at the painting of early Ste. Genevieve on pages 56-57. Ask them to make a list of the different forms of transportation that they see in the picture. If they visited Ste. Genevieve today, what kinds of transportation would they expect to see? (1.5; 1.9)

SUMMARY OF PRINCIPAL POINTS

This chapter briefly tells the familiar story of Christopher Columbus's discovery of America. It shows how the interests of European explorers led them to Missouri. Emphasis is placed on the role of the French fur traders and missionaries in starting Missouri's first European settlements. The founding and early years of the state's two oldest permanent settlements—Ste. Genevieve and St. Louis—are discussed. Auguste Chouteau, the French fur trader and cofounder of St. Louis, is featured as a Famous Missourian. A selection from Father Marquette's journal presents his observations about the American bison—an animal that was unknown to Europeans.

ANSWERS TO QUESTIONS AND EXERCISES IN THE TEXT

In Their Own Words

1. Wild cattle.

2. They were similar to French cattle, but larger. They had large heads, with horns like oxen. They also had a large piece of skin hanging down under their necks, and there was a high hump on their backs. They had a thick mane like horses, which fell over their eyes and kept them from seeing well. Their bodies were covered with a heavy coat of curly hair, like sheep's wool, but it was much stronger and thicker. Their legs were thick and short, and they could not run very fast.

3. They used them for making robes and for food.

4. Answers will vary.

Testing Yourself

1. They both wanted to find a quicker route from Europe to Asia by water. Europeans liked products such as spices (pepper, cinnamon, ginger, cloves, nutmeg), rice, figs, oranges, perfumes, silks, fine rugs, and precious stones. These things came from Asia in the East, and the trip was long and costly.

2. Nina, Pinta, Santa Maria.

3. Because he believed that he had reached the Asian East Indies.

4. Gold and silver.

5. They came for many reasons. They came to trade with the Indian people for furs, to teach the Native Americans about the Christian faith, to look for valuable metals, to make salt, and to farm.

6. People on the frontier used salt for seasoning food, preserving meat, and for curing and tanning animal skins.

7. Mostly French farmers and their African slaves who moved from settlements across the Mississippi River in Illinois.

8. Pierre Laclede established a settlement, which he named St. Louis, as a fur-trading post.

Fill in the Blanks

1. Christopher Columbus.

2. Louis Jolliet, Jacques Marquette.

3. Ste. Genevieve.

4. Auguste Chouteau.

5. fur trade.

Things to Do

1. Answers will vary. Suggestions: The Indians thought the French talked funny and their clothes were strange. They also did not think that the French were very smart because they had trouble living and getting around in the wilderness. They were interested in their guns, tools, and other implements. They were also surprised how the French could communicate using written words that were not spoken.

2. Answers will vary. Suggestions: The adventure of traveling down the Mighty Mississippi, meeting the Indians and learning more about them, and seeing strange new animals and plants.

3. Answers will vary.

4. Answers will vary. Suggestions: Sometimes the Indians they traded with for food and furs moved away. Some of the settlements were too far from any place where they could get supplies. It cost too much money to transport goods to such remote places. It cost too much to live there, and they could not make a profit.

Using a Time Line

1. Columbus, DeSoto, Marquette and Jolliet, LaSalle, the founding of Ste. Genevieve, and the founding of St. Louis.

2. Louis Jolliet could have met LaSalle, since both were French and lived about the same time. Christopher Columbus lived too many years before Jolliet to have met him, and Auguste Chouteau was born too many years after Jolliet to have known him.

CHAPTER 4

LIFE IN FRENCH MISSOURI

What All Students Should Know

The Guiding Questions listed below are correlated with the text and intended to assist teachers and curriculum designers with the development of unit and lesson plans. The applicable Show-Me Knowledge Standards for Social Studies are referenced in parentheses at the end of each question. A listing of those standards can be found on page 5 of this Guide.

1. How was life in French Missouri different from life today? (SS2; SS6; SS7)

2. Besides the French, what other groups of people also lived in early Missouri? What were some of the reasons for Missouri's cultural diversity? How did early Missouri's cultural makeup resemble the cultural diversity of the United States today? (SS2; SS6; SS7)

3. How did the diverse people in early Missouri work together and learn from each other? Did their differences sometimes lead to misunderstanding and problems? (SS2; SS6; SS7)

What All Students Should Be Able to Do

1.1. Develop questions and ideas to initiate and refine research.

1.2. Conduct research to answer questions and evaluate information and ideas.

1.3. Design and conduct field and laboratory investigations to study nature and society.

1.4. Use technological tools and other resources to locate, select, and organize information.

1.5. Comprehend and evaluate written, visual, and oral presentations and works.

1.6. Discover and evaluate patterns and relationships in information.

1.7. Evaluate the accuracy of information and ideas and the reliability of their sources.

1.8. Organize data, information, and ideas into useful forms for analysis or presentation.

1.9. Identify, analyze, and compare the institutions, traditions, and art forms of past and present societies.

1.10. Apply acquired information, ideas, and skills to different contexts.

2.1. Plan and make written, oral, and visual presentations for a variety of purposes and audiences.

2.2. Review and revise communications to improve accuracy and clarity.

2.3. Exchange information, questions, and ideas while recognizing the perspectives of others.

2.4. Present perceptions and ideas regarding works of the arts, humanities, and sciences.

2.5. Perform or produce works in the fine and practical arts.

2.7. Use technological tools to exchange information and ideas.

3.1. Identify problems and define their scope and elements.

3.2. Develop and apply strategies based on ways others have prevented or solved problems.

3.3. Develop and apply strategies based on one's own experiences in preventing or solving problems.

3.4. Evaluate the processes used in recognizing and solving problems.

3.5. Reason inductively from a set of specific facts and deductively from general premises.

3.6. Examine problems and proposed solutions from multiple perspectives.

3.7. Evaluate the extent to which a strategy addresses the problem.

3.8. Assess costs, benefits, and other consequences of proposed solutions.

4.1. Explain reasoning and identify information used to support decisions.

4.2. Understand and apply the rights and responsibilities of citizenship in Missouri and in the United States.

4.3. Analyze the duties and responsibilities of individuals in societies.

4.4. Recognize and practice honesty and integrity in academic work.

4.5. Develop, monitor, and revise plans of action to meet deadlines and accomplish those tasks.

Sample Learning Activities

The applicable Show-Me Process Standards are referenced in parentheses.

* Invite the students to generate questions about life in French Missouri that might interest them. Assist them in refining those questions for use in their research and study—the Guiding Questions should help facilitate that process. (1.1)

* Ask students to pretend that they are a boy or girl living in French Missouri. Have them write a letter to someone their age living today describing their community and some of the things they do. (1.2; 1.5; 1.9; 2.1)

* Talk about how pictures can be useful sources of information. Stress

the importance of carefully examining illustrations in books. Ask the students to look at the painting of early Ste. Genevieve on pages 56-57 and instruct them to look for clues that might indicate that this was a painting of an early French settlement. This activity would lend itself to the Think/Pair/Share learning strategy. As a follow-up you might invite the students to choose another of the illustrations in chapters 3 and 4 and write a short paragraph on what they see. (1.2; 1.5; 1.9; 2.1; 2.4)

* Discuss how life in French Missouri might have been different for the many African Americans who lived there. You can use this opportunity to introduce the subject of slavery and have a discussion about how people sometimes treat other people badly. You should also make it a point to stress the important contributions that African Americans made to the growth and development of early Missouri. (1.1; 1.2; 1.6; 1.9; 2.3; 3.1; 3.6)

* Ask students to discuss why Jeanette Fourchet has become famous. What special problems did she have to face? How might the fact that she was both a woman and African American have made things more difficult for her? Ask them to explain what they believe made her so successful in spite of the disadvantages that she faced. This is also a good time to remind students that all African Americans were not slaves. (1.5; 1.6; 1.9; 2.3; 3.1; 3.6)

* Have the students draw a mural depicting scenes from life in French Missouri. Remind them to include pictures showing the different kinds of people who lived there and some of their activities. (1.2; 1.5; 1.9; 2.1; 2.5)

* Have the students make a chart listing the different activities and responsibilities of men and women in French Missouri. They might include a separate column for children. (1.2; 1.6; 1.8)

* From the food and dishes mentioned in this chapter as favorites of the French settlers, guide the class in making a menu the French settlers might have served. (1.2; 1.9)

* View with the class the segment on the Bolduc House in "A Meeting of Cultures," video no. 4 in the Finding Missouri series. Before showing the video you should have the students generate questions about early French houses. After they have seen the video ask them to describe what they learned about French houses. Have them compare the photographs of the Bolduc House in their textbook with the film images. (1.1; 1.2; 1.4; 1.5; 1.9)

* The class might enjoy drawing pictures or making a model of the Bolduc House. (1.2; 1.9; 2.1; 2.5)

* Invite someone who speaks French to visit the class and to teach the students a few simple French words. This might also be a good time to talk about the value of learning to speak a second language. (1.9)

SUMMARY OF PRINCIPAL POINTS

The first European settlers in Missouri were French. They were joined by the African slaves they brought with them and by the Native Americans who already lived there. These red, white, and black settlers lived together in Missouri's early French settlements. After 1800, new settlers coming from the United States outnumbered the French. Still, the French made important contributions to Missouri's early development and culture. Aspects of French life in Missouri discussed include villages, houses, clothing, cooking, family life, schools, religious beliefs, recreational activities, farming practices, fur trading, and mining activities. Attention is devoted to the important role of African Americans during the French period and to the relationship between the French settlers and their Indian neighbors. Some consideration is given to the differences between the customs of the French and those of the newly arriving Americans. The story of the Valle family of Ste. Genevieve is included, and Jeanette Fourchet, a free black woman from St. Louis, is the featured Famous Missourian. A brief passage from Henry Marie Brackenridge's writings describes his boyhood experiences learning French in Ste. Genevieve.

ANSWERS TO QUESTIONS AND EXERCISES IN THE TEXT

In Their Own Words

1. Answers will vary. Suggested: He was probably homesick, lonely, and afraid at first.

2. By listening and by learning to read and spell French words at school.

3. In a few months he knew French better than English.

4. Henry had to go to school to relearn English after he returned home.

5. Answers will vary.

Things to Do

1. Suggested: St. Louis, Ste. Genevieve, Cape Girardeau, Bonne Terre, St. Clair, Beaufort, Desloge, Portageville, St. Charles, Versailles, Auxvasse, Paris, Creve Coeur, Des Peres, Duquesne, Frontenac, Laclede, Louisiana, Portage Des Sioux.

2. Answers will vary.

Choose the Right Words

1. French.

2. in villages.

3. logs.

4. moccasins and leather parts.

5. stews and soups.

6. gumbo.

7. Ste. Genevieve.

Things to Talk About

1. Answers will vary.

2. French merchants usually used their homes as a place of business. American merchants usually had their businesses in a separate part of town from their home. The French usually built their houses by placing logs in an upright position. Logs in houses built by American settlers were laid horizontally. The French had common fields and grazing lands for everyone to use; American settlers usually had individual farms. The French liked gumbos, stews, and soups. The Americans liked roasted and fried foods. The French liked bread made from wheat. The Americans liked corn bread. French women had more to say about business than American women. The French were mostly Catholics. The Americans were mostly Protestants. The French got along with the Indians better than the American settlers. Many French settlers earned their living as merchants, fur traders, and miners who often had to travel away from their homes, but most pioneer American settlers were farmers who stayed on their land.

True or False

1. True.

2. False. Suggested: Early French houses were different from the early houses built by American settlers.

3. False. Suggested: Most French families had several children.

4. True.

5. True.

6. True.

7. False. Suggested: Some of the African Americans in early Missouri were free people.

8. False. Suggested: Games and fun were an important part of the French settlers' lives.

CHAPTER 5

MISSOURI BECOMES A PART OF THE UNITED STATES

What All Students Should Know

The Guiding Questions listed below are correlated with the text and intended to assist teachers and curriculum designers with the development of unit and lesson plans. The applicable Show-Me Knowledge Standards for Social Studies are referenced in parentheses at the end of each question. A listing of those standards can be found on page 5 of this Guide.

1. Why did so many different nations compete to control the land that today is Missouri? (SS2; SS5; SS6; SS7)

2. What was the Declaration of Independence and why was it an important document? How did it lead to the formation of the United States? (SS1; SS2; SS3; SS6)

3. Why was the Louisiana Purchase such an important event in both Missouri history and United States history? What was it? Who were some of the people who participated in it? How did it change Missouri and the United States? What kind of changes did it bring to people who were living in the region that is today Missouri? (SS2; SS3; SS5; SS6)

4. After the Louisiana Purchase, why did many Missourians want their territory to become a state? What problem delayed statehood for Missouri? How was that problem resolved? (SS1; SS2; SS3; SS6)

5. What is a constitution? What were some good things in Missouri's first state constitution? What were some bad things in it? Have those things been changed? (SS1; SS2; SS3)

6. Why did Missourians decide to move their capital to Jefferson City? What geographic features contributed to the selection of that location? (SS6; SS7)

7. Why was the Lewis and Clark expedition so important? What was their assignment? Why was it so successful? What skills and qualities of character did Lewis and Clark and the other members of the expedition use to accomplish what they did? Why do we still celebrate the travels of Lewis and Clark today? (SS2; SS5; SS6; SS7)

What All Students Should Be Able to Do

1.1. Develop questions and ideas to initiate and refine research.

1.2. Conduct research to answer questions and evaluate information and ideas.

1.3. Design and conduct field and laboratory investigations to study nature and society.

1.4. Use technological tools and other resources to locate, select, and organize information.

1.5. Comprehend and evaluate written, visual, and oral presentations and works.

1.6. Discover and evaluate patterns and relationships in information.

1.7. Evaluate the accuracy of information and ideas and the reliability of their sources.

1.8. Organize data, information, and ideas into useful forms for analysis or presentation.

1.9. Identify, analyze, and compare the institutions, traditions, and art forms of past and present societies.

1.10. Apply acquired information, ideas, and skills to different contexts.

2.1. Plan and make written, oral, and visual presentations for a variety of purposes and audiences.

2.2. Review and revise communications to improve accuracy and clarity.

2.3. Exchange information, questions, and ideas while recognizing the perspectives of others.

2.4. Present perceptions and ideas regarding works of the arts, humanities, and sciences.

2.5. Perform or produce works in the fine and practical arts.

2.7. Use technological tools to exchange information and ideas.

3.1. Identify problems and define their scope and elements.

3.2. Develop and apply strategies based on ways others have prevented or solved problems.

3.3. Develop and apply strategies based on one's own experiences in preventing or solving problems.

3.4. Evaluate the processes used in recognizing and solving problems.

3.5. Reason inductively from a set of specific facts and deductively from general premises.

3.6. Examine problems and proposed solutions from multiple perspectives.

3.7. Evaluate the extent to which a strategy addresses the problem.

3.8. Assess costs, benefits, and other consequences of proposed solutions.

4.1. Explain reasoning and identify information used to support decisions.

4.2. Understand and apply the rights and responsibilities of citizenship in Missouri and in the United States.

4.3. Analyze the duties and responsibilities of individuals in societies.

4.4. Recognize and practice honesty and integrity in academic work.

4.5. Develop, monitor, and revise plans of action to meet deadlines and accomplish those tasks.

Sample Learning Activities

The applicable Show-Me Performance Standards are referenced in parentheses.

* Ask the students to make a list of the different countries that controlled the land now called Missouri. Look up the flags of those countries and have the students make flags representing each of those countries. (1.2; 1.4)

* Assign the students research to find out more about the Declaration

of Independence. Discuss some of the key ideas that are contained in this document. Show how it was important to the creation of American democracy. You should also note that at the time the founders stated that all people were created equal and should have the same rights, some Americans, including Thomas Jefferson, still owned slaves. Students should also understand how the Declaration of Independence was related to the American Revolutionary War. If any of the students have visited the National Archives in Washington, D.C., where the Declaration of Independence is on display, invite them to tell other members of the class about what they saw. (1.1; 1.2; 1.5; 1.9; 4.2; 4.3)

* Discuss with the students the reasons that July 4 is a national holiday. Ask them to identify the official name for this holiday-- Independence Day. Explain to them that it is the nation's birthday. The United States was officially created on July 4, 1776. Invite the students to tell the ways that they celebrate the Fourth of July. Ask them to draw pictures that celebrate American Independence. (1.9; 2.1; 4.2)

* Have the students read a biography of Thomas Jefferson. Ask them to explain why he was important in United States history and in Missouri history. Have them make a list of some of Jefferson's accomplishments. You might also want to mention that despite his greatness, Jefferson was not perfect. Like many people of his day Jefferson owned slaves. (1.2; 1.5; 1.9; 2.3)

* Conduct research about the Louisiana Purchase and its importance. Discuss how the people that were living in the Louisiana Territory might have felt when they learned that they were about to become a part of the United States. Have the students prepare a newspaper story announcing the Louisiana Purchase. (1.1; 1.2; 2.1)

* Dramatize the American offer to buy New Orleans, Napoleon's offer to sell all of Louisiana instead, and the American decision to accept his offer. (1.5; 2.1; 2.5)

* On an outline map of the United States have the students identify and color in the states that were later created from land in the Louisiana Purchase. (1.2; 1.8)

* Have the students construct a time line of important events leading up to statehood for Missouri:

      a. President Monroe approves Missouri's admission as the twenty-fourth state (1821)

      b. Declaration of Independence creates the United States of America (1776)

      c. Congress approves the Missouri Compromise (1820)

      d. The Louisiana Purchase makes Missouri a part of the United States (1803) (1.8)

* Have the students conduct research to learn more about Lewis and Clark and other members of the expedition. Ask them to prepare questions that they would like to ask various members of the expedition. Trace the route that the expedition followed. Identify the future states that Lewis and Clark passed through on their way to the Pacific. Trace their route through Missouri and identify places where they camped along the Missouri River. Have the students make a map showing some of those places. This topic is a perfect vehicle for making use of the internet to conduct research. There are many excellent web sites that contain valuable information about this expedition, including several that are listed in the text at the end of chapter 5. Students in the St. Louis area might want to visit the special Lewis and Clark exhibits at the Missouri Historical Society's History Museum. (1.1; 1.2; 1.3; 1.4; 1.5; 1.9; 2.1; 2.3)

* View with the students the segments on the Lewis and Clark expedition and Fort Osage in "Gateway West," video no. 5 in the Finding Missouri series. Before showing the video segments invite the students to generate questions about Lewis and Clark and Fort Osage. After watching the video ask the students to relate the things that they learned about each topic. (1.1; 1.2; 1.4; 1.5; 1.9)

* Explore with the students possible reasons that the expedition was a success. What were some of the hardships that members of the expedition faced? Ask the students to identify the skills and personal qualities that were required. Have each student write a short paragraph on leadership, such as "Some Things a Leader Should Know," "The Troubles a Leader Has," or "Why I Would Like to Be a Leader." (1.5; 3.2)

* Dramatize the arrival of Lewis and Clark at the Pacific Ocean. (2.5)

* Relate to the students the process for becoming a state. Explain that a territorial government is formed first. Providing the United States Congress approves, when a territory has enough people (sixty thousand) and a constitution has been written, the territory can become a state. (1.5)

* Have the students do research about the Missouri Compromise. What were the issues that were keeping Missouri out of the Union? Discuss what is meant by a compromise. Show how it is sometimes necessary to reach a compromise to settle a political disagreement. Whose interests were not taken into consideration when the Missouri Compromise was approved? (1.1; 1.5; 1.9; 2.1; 3.4)

* View with the students "A State Is Born," video no. 6 in the Finding Missouri series. The entire video should interest fourth graders, though you may want to view the segments on Missouri Becomes a State and Missouri's First State Capitol separately. The complete video is eleven

minutes long. Before watching the video invite the students to formulate questions and use them to guide the discussion about the video and about the Missouri Compromise. (1.1; 1.2; 1.4; 1.5; 1.9)

SUMMARY OF PRINCIPAL POINTS

European interest in the Mississippi River valley led to international rivalries for control of this rich region, which included Missouri. Later the area west of the Mississippi River, commonly called the Louisiana Territory, passed from France to Spain, back to France, and finally to the United States. When Spanish officials governed Louisiana, few Spaniards settled in Missouri. At first, most new settlers continued to come from the French settlements east of the Mississippi River. Later Spain permitted Americans to settle in Missouri. Daniel and Rebecca Boone came to Missouri with members of their family during the Spanish period. The Americans made up a majority of the residents of Missouri by 1803, when the United States purchased the Louisiana Territory.

After the Louisiana Territory became a part of the United States even more Americans came to Missouri. With its growing population, Missouri sought to become a state. A dispute over slavery kept Missouri out of the Union for two years. The Missouri Compromise settled this disagreement. Missouri was admitted into the Union in 1821. Missourians had to write a constitution for their state. St. Charles was chosen to be the state capital, until a new capital city could be built near the center of the state. In 1826 the capital was moved to Jefferson City, which was named for Thomas Jefferson. Explorers Meriwether Lewis and William Clark are profiled as Famous Missourians. William Clark's journal presents some of the things he observed during their journey to the Pacific.

ADDITIONAL INFORMATION

The various transfers of the Mississippi valley from one nation to another often confuse students. The following account may help clarify the situation.

Spain tried to establish its claim over the Mississippi valley as a result of Hernando de Soto's expedition of 1539-1542. But it was France that established the first effective European claim in central North America, through the journeys of Jolliet and Marquette and La Salle. As you know, La Salle named the Mississippi River valley Louisiana and claimed it for France. Limited French settlement started on the east bank of the Mississippi shortly before 1700.

A major war, known as the French and Indian War (1754-1763), which involved the most important European countries, caused France to lose control of the region. France was forced to transfer all of the lands west of the Mississippi River to Spain and all of the lands east of the Mississippi River to England. After 1763 the term "Louisiana" generally referred to the area between the Mississippi River and the Rocky Mountains.

Even though Spain controlled Louisiana, few Spaniards migrated there. French people continued to come from east of the Mississippi to live in Louisiana. They felt more comfortable under Spanish rule than under English rule.

The land east of the Mississippi passed from England to the newly created United States of America under the terms of the treaty that ended the American Revolutionary War in 1783.

Near the close of the 1700s, Napoleon Bonaparte came to power in France. Under his leadership France again became a major power in Europe. Napoleon planned to reestablish a great empire in the New World. He secured Louisiana from Spain in exchange for territory in Italy.

As a part of his New World venture, Napoleon sent an expedition to reestablish French control over the colony of Santo Domingo. A revolt there had placed control of the colony in the hands of rebellious slaves. To Napoleon's surprise, the slaves held the island against the French army, which was decimated by disease. Without a strong army in the New World, Napoleon was forced to give up his plans to restore French control in the Americas. Napoleon now turned his attention to new conquests in Europe.

In need of money for his new European campaign, Napoleon offered to sell the entire Louisiana Territory to the United States. Under President Thomas Jefferson the United States purchased the Louisiana Territory in 1803 for fifteen million dollars. The Louisiana Purchase nearly doubled the size of the United States and placed Missouri under American control.

ANSWERS TO QUESTIONS AND EXERCISES IN THE TEXT

In Their Own Words

1. Watching for Indians, wild animals, fruit, berries, and nuts, other kinds of plants and flowers, stray horses, the weather, mosquitoes, and what he ate for his birthday celebration.

2. Meet and confer with Indians, hunt animals for food, gather wild fruit, berries, and nuts, recover stray horses, and cook. They also had to man the boats to move them up the river and fix the vessels when they needed repairs. President Jefferson had also asked them to keep records of their travels, make maps, and collect scientific information.

3. He ate a large piece of fat deer meat, a beaver tail, and a dessert made of several kinds of berries.

4. Beaver, caught, gathering ordered, venison, cherries, quality, evening, mosquitoes, very troublesome, prairies, raspberries, gooseberries, hazel nuts, flowers, botanist, and naturalist.

Testing Yourself

1. The Louisiana Purchase made Missouri a part of the United States.

2. French, Spanish, American.

3. They were promised free land and no taxes. The land was also good for farming and hunting.

4. Kentucky, Tennessee, Virginia, North Carolina.

5. To make the capital city closer to people in all parts of the state. Nobody had to travel too far. Many people could also use the Missouri River to get there.

Matching Partners

1-b, 2-c, 3-a, 4-d

Things to Talk About

1. Answers will vary. Suggested: They were sad and afraid that they would have to change their way of life. They knew that the Americans spoke another language and had different kinds of government and religion. They also thought that they were not as easygoing as the French.

2. Because it protects the people's rights. These rights include freedom of speech, press, and religion, and the right to have a fair trial with a jury. It sets limits on the government's power to restrict those rights.

3. Answers will vary.

Things to Do

1. All or parts of Louisiana, Arkansas, Iowa, Minnesota, North Dakota, South Dakota, Nebraska, Kansas, Oklahoma, Montana, Wyoming, Colorado, Texas.

2. Answers will vary.

3. France loses Louisiana to Spain (1763), Declaration of Independence (1776), Louisiana is bought by the United States (1803), and Missouri becomes a state (1821).

CHAPTER 6

LIFE ON THE FRONTIER

What All Students Should Know

The Guiding Questions listed below are correlated with the text and intended to assist teachers and curriculum designers with the development of unit and lesson plans. The applicable Show-Me Knowledge Standards for Social Studies are referenced in parentheses at the end of each question. A listing of those standards can be found on page 5 of this Guide.

1. How was pioneer life in Missouri after it became a state different from life in Missouri today? (SS2; SS6; SS7)

2. How did people on the frontier work together to accomplish tasks and to have fun? (SS2; SS6)

3. Why did fewer settlers choose to live in the Ozarks before the Civil War? How did geographic features affect settlement in the Ozarks? What special problems did Ozark pioneers face? Why did some individuals such as Margaret Gilmore Kelso prefer living in the Ozarks? (SS2; SS5; SS7)

What All Students Should Be Able to Do

1.1. Develop questions and ideas to initiate and refine research.

1.2. Conduct research to answer questions and evaluate information and ideas.

1.3. Design and conduct field and laboratory investigations to study nature and society.

1.4. Use technological tools and other resources to locate, select, and organize information.

1.5. Comprehend and evaluate written, visual, and oral presentations and works.

1.6. Discover and evaluate patterns and relationships in information.

1.7. Evaluate the accuracy of information and ideas and the reliability of their sources.

1.8. Organize data, information, and ideas into useful forms for analysis or presentation.

1.9. Identify, analyze, and compare the institutions, traditions, and art forms of past and present societies.

1.10. Apply acquired information, ideas, and skills to different contexts.

2.1. Plan and make written, oral, and visual presentations for a variety of purposes and audiences.

2.2. Review and revise communications to improve accuracy and clarity.

2.3. Exchange information, questions, and ideas while recognizing the perspectives of others.

2.4. Present perceptions and ideas regarding works of the arts, humanities, and sciences.

2.5. Perform or produce works in the fine and practical arts.

2.7. Use technological tools to exchange information and ideas.

3.1. Identify problems and define their scope and elements.

3.2. Develop and apply strategies based on ways others have prevented or solved problems.

3.3. Develop and apply strategies based on one's own experiences in preventing or solving problems.

3.4. Evaluate the processes used in recognizing and solving problems.

3.5. Reason inductively from a set of specific facts and deductively from general premises.

3.6. Examine problems and proposed solutions from multiple perspectives.

3.7. Evaluate the extent to which a strategy addresses the problem.

3.8. Assess costs, benefits, and other consequences of proposed solutions.

4.1. Explain reasoning and identify information used to support decisions.

4.2. Understand and apply the rights and responsibilities of citizenship in Missouri and in the United States.

4.3. Analyze the duties and responsibilities of individuals in societies.

4.4. Recognize and practice honesty and integrity in academic work.

4.5. Develop, monitor, and revise plans of action to meet deadlines and accomplish those tasks.

Sample Learning Activities

The applicable Show-Me Performance Standards are referenced in parentheses.

* Invite the students to generate questions about pioneer life that interest them. Assist them in refining those questions and use them to guide their research and study. (1.1)

* Conduct research about pioneer life in Missouri using information from different kinds of sources (e.g., books, primary sources [eyewitness or firsthand accounts], illustrations, and videos). Discuss with the students how to use the different kinds of sources. (1.1; 1.2; 1.4; 1.5; 1.6; 1.7)

* Ask the students to look carefully at the picture of the frontier farm on page 115 and make a list of the different activities it shows. Invite them to discuss those activities and their purpose. (1.2; 1.5; 1.9)

* Read Margaret Gilmore Kelso's account of pioneer life in the Ozarks. Discuss with them what is meant by a primary source (a firsthand or eyewitness account) and explain how this is different from an account in a textbook or an encyclopedia. Discuss with them the advantages and disadvantages of using primary sources. Ask the children to compare Kelso's childhood experiences with their own. Talk about how houses and schools then were different from those today. (1.2; 1.7; 1.9)

* Have the students log on to one of the web sites listed at the end of the chapter and see what new information they can find there. (1.2; 1.4)

* Ask the students to discuss the experiments of Dr. Beaumont and

Dr. Sappington. Then discuss with them how medical treatment and health care services were different from those of today. (1.5; 1.9; 2.3)

* Have the students compare information from the various sources that they have consulted. Guide them in making generalizations regarding the early settlers—how they built their houses, got their food, obtained the clothing, and made their tools. Have them write down their conclusions in a chart similar to the one they made about the Indians for chapter 1. (1.5; 1.6; 1.7; 1.8; 1.9)

* Compare the way the early settlers lived with the way Indian people lived, as written in the charts that they have made. Talk about the ways that their customs were alike and the ways they were different. Invite the students to decide what they believe is the most important difference. Ask them to consider if the settlers should have expected the Indians to give up their lands and their ways of living. (1.5; 1.6; 1.9; 3.6)

* Ask the students to make a chart comparing life on a pioneer farm with life on a farm today. Divide the chart into two columns: "Pioneer Farm" and "Farm of Today." Have them list examples in each column. In the first column they should tell something about pioneer farm life, and in the second column with life today. (1.5; 1.6; 1.8; 1.9)

* Have each student pretend that he or she lives on a pioneer farm on the frontier. Let each student write a letter to an imaginary friend in the East telling about the chores he or she does each day, how the family home was built, what kind of furniture it has in it, what school is like on the frontier, how the family gets its food, and so forth. (1.5; 1.9; 2.1)

* Have the students read a book about a famous pioneer such as Daniel Boone and report on it to the members of the class. (1.2; 2.1)

* The students might enjoy an old-fashioned spelling bee. Choose words from this book. (1.10)

SUMMARY OF PRINCIPAL POINTS

The pioneer settlers looked for an area with a good water supply, rich soil, and good timber. It took hard work to establish a home on the frontier. Trees had to be cut down, cabins had to be built, and crops had to be planted. People had to grow or make most of the things they needed. All members of a family had to do their part. The Coles were an early Missouri pioneer family. On the Missouri frontier Native Americans and pioneer settlers often lived in the same area. They often remained on friendly terms, but sometimes the attempts to take over Indian lands led to trouble. Early schools were primitive, but Missourians believed in education and did what they could to provide schools for their children. The pioneers welcomed the early circuit riders and established regular churches as soon as there were enough people to support them.

Missouri pioneers found opportunities for fun and recreation. Without the recreational opportunities of a well-established community and with little time to waste, the pioneers often combined business with pleasure. The people's interest in public speaking and in books is also discussed. Special attention is given to pioneer life in the Missouri Ozarks. Margaret Gilmore Kelso describes pioneer life in the Ozarks in her own words. The Catholic nun Saint Rose Philippine Duchesne is the featured Famous Missourian in this chapter.

ANSWERS TO QUESTIONS AND EXERCISES IN THE TEXT

In Their Own Words

1. Fine rich land [in some places], beautiful scenery, many fine springs, rivers, and lakes with a lot of fish.

2. One room, with little equipment. There were slabs for benches, there were no blackboards, and there was a little square opening in one wall to let in the light.

3. Small log cabins. Margaret Kelso's family's cabin had dirt floors, a fireplace, and a bed frame made with poles stuck in holes bored into the log walls.

4. Answers will vary.

Testing Yourself

1. They came because the soil was rich, because there was plenty of timber, water, and wild game; because land was cheap, and because they wanted to build new lives.

2. Ax, rifle, and perhaps hoes, shovels, or a plow.

3. Corn bread, hominy, milk, butter, beef, pork, wild game, fish, wild fruits and berries, garden vegetables and fruits, and maple sugar.

4. By drying fruits and vegetables, and curing meat with salt.

5. They helped to build a cabin, house, or barn, helped with the harvest of crops, helped with sewing, and also helped take care of families and children when someone was sick.

6. The thin, rocky soil was not good for raising crops, and the steep, tree-covered hills made travel more difficult.

Things to Do

1. Gun, seed, cow, ax, spinning wheel, plow.

2. Motion picture projector, drinking fountain, electric clock, fire alarm, gymnasium.

3. Answers will vary.

Things to Talk About

1. Answers will vary.

2. Cotton and flax were grown, and wool was cut from sheep. The fibers were

spun into thread and then were woven into cloth on a loom. Finally the cloth was sewn by hand into garments to be worn. (Garments were also made from the skins of animals.)

3. Children were needed to help with many chores on the farm. They might work in the garden, chop wood for the fireplace, take care of farm animals, milk the cows, help harvest the crops, and many other things.

4. Because it grew well in Missouri, it was easy to store, and it could be made into many different kinds of food such as corn bread and hominy. Corn was also excellent feed for the farm animals. Many pioneers used corn to make whiskey.

5. If a country is to be run by the people, the people must be able to make wise decisions. Schools help educate people to be good citizens.

6. Answers will vary.

CHAPTER 7
EARLY TRAVEL

What All Students Should Know

The Guiding Questions listed below are correlated with the text and intended to assist teachers and curriculum designers with the development of unit and lesson plans. The applicable Show-Me Knowledge Standards for Social Studies are referenced in parentheses at the end of each question. A listing of those standards can be found on page 5 of this Guide.

1. What were the advantages and disadvantages of traveling by water and over land in early Missouri? Which did most early Missourians prefer? Why? (SS2; SS5)

2. What improvements occurred in the forms of water transportation? How did changes in technology make traveling by water easier? (SS2; SS5)

3. Why did the railroad become such an important method of transportation? What were the advantages and disadvantages of this form of transportation? (SS2; SS5)

What All Students Should Be Able to Do

1.1. Develop questions and ideas to initiate and refine research.

1.2. Conduct research to answer questions and evaluate information and ideas.

1.3. Design and conduct field and laboratory investigations to study nature and society.

1.4. Use technological tools and other resources to locate, select, and organize information.

1.5. Comprehend and evaluate written, visual, and oral presentations and works.

1.6. Discover and evaluate patterns and relationships in information.

1.7. Evaluate the accuracy of information and ideas and the reliability of their sources.

1.8. Organize data, information, and ideas into useful forms for analysis or presentation.

1.9. Identify, analyze, and compare the institutions, traditions, and art forms of past and present societies.

1.10. Apply acquired information, ideas, and skills to different contexts.

2.1. Plan and make written, oral, and visual presentations for a variety of purposes and audiences.

2.2. Review and revise communications to improve accuracy and clarity.

2.3. Exchange information, questions, and ideas while recognizing the perspectives of others.

2.4. Present perceptions and ideas regarding works of the arts, humanities, and sciences.

2.5. Perform or produce works in the fine and practical arts.

2.7. Use technological tools to exchange information and ideas.

3.1. Identify problems and define their scope and elements.

3.2. Develop and apply strategies based on ways others have prevented or solved problems.

3.3. Develop and apply strategies based on one's own experiences in preventing or solving problems.

3.4. Evaluate the processes used in recognizing and solving problems.

3.5. Reason inductively from a set of specific facts and deductively from general premises.

3.6. Examine problems and proposed solutions from multiple perspectives.

3.7. Evaluate the extent to which a strategy addresses the problem.

3.8. Assess costs, benefits, and other consequences of proposed solutions.

4.1. Explain reasoning and identify information used to support decisions.

4.2. Understand and apply the rights and responsibilities of citizenship in Missouri and in the United States.

4.3. Analyze the duties and responsibilities of individuals in societies.

4.4. Recognize and practice honesty and integrity in academic work.

4.5. Develop, monitor, and revise plans of action to meet deadlines and accomplish those tasks.

Sample Learning Activities

The applicable Show-Me Knowledge Standards are referenced in parentheses.

* Invite the students to generate questions about early transportation that interest them. Assist them in refining them and use them to guide their research and study on the topic—the Guiding Questions should facilitate the process. (1.1)

* Have the students collect or draw pictures of different kinds of early riverboats. The class might then make a large mural depicting the development of water transportation. (1.2; 2.1; 2.5)

* Some of the students might like to make models of early river craft. (2.1; 2.5)

* In class discussion, let the students suggest by which routes the following people might have come to Missouri: people from Europe, people from New Orleans, people from Ohio, people from the southern United States. Use maps and globes to show possible routes. (1.2; 1.4; 1.6)

* Have some member or members of the class make a report on Mark Twain as a steamboat pilot. (1.2; 2.1)

* Conduct research to learn more about the steamboat *Arabia* and its recovery. The Steamboat *Arabia* Museum web site is a good source of information. Invite the students to discuss possible problems that might be involved with recovering a buried steamboat. (1.2; 1.4; 1.6)

* Arrange for a visit to a museum that features transportation exhibits such as the Steamboat *Arabia* Museum, the History Museum in St. Louis, or the St. Louis Museum of Transportation. (1.2; 1.3)

* Assign students to conduct research about early railroads and how their construction affected Missouri cities and towns. (1.2; 1.6)

SUMMARY OF PRINCIPAL POINTS

This chapter emphasizes the importance of transportation for everyday living. It shows how improved kinds of transportation enabled the state to grow and develop and enabled people to enjoy a better standard of living. There is a chronological account that traces the various means of transportation from the days of the crude river raft to the introduction of the steam railroads. The development of more modern types of transportation is discussed in later chapters. Samuel Clemens, the great American writer who was once a Mississippi River steamboat pilot, is the Famous Missourian in this chapter. The story of the sinking and the recovery of the Steamboat *Arabia* is a special feature in this chapter.

ANSWERS TO QUESTIONS AND EXERCISES IN THE TEXT

Testing Yourself

1. Automobiles, trucks, diesel trains, airplanes, space craft.

2. There were few real roads. Rivers were the easiest way to travel a long distance.

3. Ice, floods, floating logs, snags, fast currents.

4. Dugout, canoe, flatboat, keelboat.

5. A keelboat was stronger and better built and their shape made it easier for them to travel up a river than on a flatboat.

6. The steamboat had an engine that turned paddlewheels that pushed the boat through the water at a faster speed. It was also larger and could carry more people and heavier loads.

7. They were short, rough, full of ruts and tree stumps, and often muddy. Later, plank roads were built, but the planks soon warped or rotted and made the road unusable.

8. Railroad tracks could be laid almost anywhere. Once they had been laid, the tracks were easy to maintain and long lasting. Steam engines could also pull larger and heavier loads more rapidly than other types of land transportation.

Choose the Right Words

1. river.
2. river.
3. keelboat.
4. steamboat.
5. pilot.
6. wagons.
7. "road bees."

Things to Talk About

1. Answers will vary.
2. Answers will vary.
3. Floating ice, logs and snags, sandbars, shallow channels, bad currents.

CHAPTER 8

MISSOURI AND THE WEST

What All Students Should Know

The Guiding Questions listed below are correlated with the text and intended to assist teachers and curriculum designers with the development of unit and lesson plans. The applicable Show-Me Knowledge Standards for Social Studies are referenced in parentheses at the end of each question. A listing of those standards can be found on page 5 of this Guide.

1. How did Missouri's location help it to become the Gateway to the West? Why did so many western trails begin in Missouri? (SS2; SS5)

2. Why did so many people want to go to the West? What were they expecting to find? What were some popular places in the West that attracted settlers? (SS2; SS4; SS5; SS6; SS7)

3. Who were some Missourians who played important roles in the exploration and settlement of the American West? (SS2; SS6)

4. What methods of transportation were available to people who were traveling to the West before the Civil War? What were some of the major problems that western travelers were likely to encounter? (SS2)

5. What was the Pony Express? What Missouri city did it help make famous? What caused it to go out of business? (SS2; SS4; SS5; SS7)

What All Students Should Be Able to Do

1.1. Develop questions and ideas to initiate and refine research.

1.2. Conduct research to answer questions and evaluate information and ideas.

1.3. Design and conduct field and laboratory investigations to study nature and society.

1.4. Use technological tools and other resources to locate, select, and organize information.

1.5. Comprehend and evaluate written, visual, and oral presentations and works.

1.6. Discover and evaluate patterns and relationships in information.

1.7. Evaluate the accuracy of information and ideas and the reliability of their sources.

1.8. Organize data, information, and ideas into useful forms for analysis or presentation.

1.9. Identify, analyze, and compare the institutions, traditions, and art forms of past and present societies.

1.10. Apply acquired information, ideas, and skills to different contexts.

2.1. Plan and make written, oral, and visual presentations for a variety of purposes and audiences.

2.2. Review and revise communications to improve accuracy and clarity.

2.3. Exchange information, questions, and ideas while recognizing the perspectives of others.

2.4. Present perceptions and ideas regarding works of the arts, humanities, and sciences.

2.5. Perform or produce works in the fine and practical arts.

2.7. Use technological tools to exchange information and ideas.

3.1. Identify problems and define their scope and elements.

3.2. Develop and apply strategies based on ways others have prevented or solved problems.

3.3. Develop and apply strategies based on one's own experiences in preventing or solving problems.

3.4. Evaluate the processes used in recognizing and solving problems.

3.5. Reason inductively from a set of specific facts and deductively from general premises.

3.6. Examine problems and proposed solutions from multiple perspectives.

3.7. Evaluate the extent to which a strategy addresses the problem.

3.8. Assess costs, benefits, and other consequences of proposed solutions.

4.1. Explain reasoning and identify information used to support decisions.

4.2. Understand and apply the rights and responsibilities of citizenship in Missouri and in the United States.

4.3. Analyze the duties and responsibilities of individuals in societies.

4.4. Recognize and practice honesty and integrity in academic work.

4.5. Develop, monitor, and revise plans of action to meet deadlines and accomplish those tasks.

Sample Learning Activities

The applicable Show-Me Performance Standards are referenced in parentheses.

* With the students trace the routes of the Santa Fe, Oregon, and California trails shown on the map on page 157. Discuss how geographic features affected the locations of these trails. Why was Missouri the starting place for all three of these trails? (1.4; 1.6)

* Review once again with the students the cardinal directions—north, south, east, and west. Then discuss northeast, northwest, southeast, and southwest. From looking at the map on page 157, ask them to identify the direction they would be heading on each of the trails shown on the map after they left Missouri. (1.4; 1.6)

* With the students compare the 1850 map on page 157 with a map of the United States today. Ask them to name the states west of the

Mississippi River that had joined the Union by 1850. Supply each member of the class with an outline map of the United States. Have them draw the Santa Fe, Oregon, and California trails on their maps. Have them label the names of the states that joined the Union after 1850. Then ask them to make a list for each of the trails with the names of any states that they would have passed through that had not yet been admitted to the Union. (1.4; 1.6; 1.8)

* Invite the students to generate a list of questions about the Santa Fe Trail that interest them. View with the class the segment on William Becknell in "Coming Through: Missourians Explore Trails West," in video no. 8 in the Finding Missouri series. After watching the video discuss with the students why the Santa Fe trail was so important to Missouri and any other matters that interest them. (1.2; 1.4; 1.5; 1.9)

* Why did Charles Orrick need a passport when he decided to travel to Santa Fe in 1845? Would someone from Missouri need a passport to travel to Santa Fe today? Why not? When do you need a passport for travel? Ask if any of the students or their parents have a passport. If so, perhaps their parents might bring it to class to show it to the students. (1.2; 1.10)

* Conduct research with the students to find out what travel conditions would have been like on a wagon train that was traveling west in 1850. Ask them to speculate about possible dangers or problems that they might have faced during their journey west. (1.1; 1.2; 1.5; 1.8)

* Ask the students to prepare a list of essential items that they would have needed to make a trip to California in 1850. Have them compare their lists and answer questions from the classmates about the things they planned to take. Caution them about the dangers of overpacking or taking too many heavy items that might slow down their progress or cause them to fall behind. When their lists are completed have them draw pictures of the things that they planned to take with them. (1.2; 2.1; 2.3)

* Pretend that you are a boy or girl in Independence, Missouri, with your family waiting to depart for California in 1850. Write to a friend in the East describing some of the things that you had seen in Independence and telling about your family's preparations for the journey to California. You should also explain why your family has decided to move to California. (1.2; 1.5; 1.9; 2.1)

* Have the students identify three major problems that families traveling west on the Oregon trail often encountered. (1.2; 1.5; 1.9)

* Ask the students to speculate about the prices of goods in St. Louis, Independence, and California during the days of the Gold Rush. Which would have had the highest prices? Which would have had the lowest prices? Why? (1.2; 1.6)

* Assign the students to read biographies of famous western explorers and pioneers. Have them report what they learned with members of the class. Then ask the class to decide what skills and qualities a successful pioneer or explorer needed. Have them write a job description listing the qualifications that the leader of a western expedition needed. (1.2; 1.5; 1.6; 2.1; 2.3)

* Discuss the contributions to westward settlement made by James P. Beckwourth and Hiram Young. What added problems did they have to overcome? (1.2; 1.5; 1.6; 1.9)

* Ask the students to decide if they would have been interested in applying for a job as a rider for the Pony Express. Discuss the pros and cons of the job. (1.5; 1.6; 2.3)

* If there are any historic sites related to western expansion in your community, arrange for the class to visit them. Provide as much background information as possible before the trip. (1.2; 1.3)

* As a class project the students might make a large mural on westward expansion for the classroom. (1.6; 1.8; 1.9; 2.5)

SUMMARY OF PRINCIPAL POINTS

Missouri played a crucial role in the settlement and development of the American West. Missouri was the starting place for many people traveling west. It also served as a warehouse for western products, and many famous western explorers and pioneers came from Missouri. This chapter traces early Missouri's contributions to western exploration and the fur trade. Missouri's role in the Santa Fe trade, the settlement of Texas and the Southwest, the gold rush, the settlement of Oregon and California, and the development of western transportation are all also discussed. The Pony Express is highlighted. The African American mountain man James P. Beckwourth is the featured Famous Missourian. David McCausland's letter to Governor John C. Edwards requesting a passport for a friend who is planning to travel to Santa Fe is the featured document in this chapter.

ANSWERS TO QUESTIONS AND EXERCISES IN THE TEXT

In Their Own Words

1. A passport is a form of identification that governments issue to citizens of their country. It allows those citizens to travel in foreign countries.

2. To trade.

3. That he was a reliable and responsible person and that McCausland would consider it a favor from his friend the governor.

4. Santa Fe is now a part of the United States and not in another country.

46

Testing Yourself

1. St. Louis.

2. Beaver, otter, mink, fox, buffalo, bear, deer.

3. Cotton and woolen cloth, iron pots and pans, tools, knives, and mirrors.

4. Furs, horses, burros, mules, and silver.

5. Independence, St. Joseph, and Westport (now a part of Kansas City).

6. To carry the mail from St. Joseph to California. The new telegraph system offered a faster and cheaper way to send messages to California.

Things to Talk About

1. A profit is any money that is left after all of the expenses of operating a business have been paid. The desire to earn a profit is what causes people to invest their time and money in a business. The Santa Fe traders were able to make a profit because the goods and money they brought back from Santa Fe were worth more than the goods they had taken there for trading. People in Santa Fe were willing to pay more for the goods from Missouri because they were scarce in the Southwest.

2. There were people in the West who spoke those languages. Travelers and people doing business there needed to be able to talk with persons who did not speak English. Since he spoke several languages, Carson could serve as an interpreter. Being able to speak more than one language is even more important today because more and more people travel and do business in all parts of the world.

Describing People

1-a; 2-d; 3-e; 4-b; 5-c

CHAPTER 9
A GROWING STATE

What All Students Should Know

The Guiding Questions listed below are correlated with the text and intended to assist teachers and curriculum designers with the development of unit and lesson plans. The applicable Show-Me Knowledge Standards for Social Studies are referenced in parentheses at the end of each question. A listing of those standards can be found on page 5 of this Guide.

1. How did new settlers add to Missouri's cultural diversity? Where did they come from? Why did they come? (SS2; SS4; SS5; SS6)

2. How did these new settlers contribute to Missouri's growth and development? (SS2; SS6)

3. How and why was Missouri changing in the years before the Civil War? (SS2; SS6; SS7)

4. How did Missourians take part in running their government before the Civil War? Which Missourians did not get to participate in making those decisions? (SS1; SS2; SS3)

What All Students Should Be Able to Do

1.1. Develop questions and ideas to initiate and refine research.

1.2. Conduct research to answer questions and evaluate information and ideas.

1.3. Design and conduct field and laboratory investigations to study nature and society.

1.4. Use technological tools and other resources to locate, select, and organize information.

1.5. Comprehend and evaluate written, visual, and oral presentations and works.

1.6. Discover and evaluate patterns and relationships in information.

1.7. Evaluate the accuracy of information and ideas and the reliability of their sources.

1.8. Organize data, information, and ideas into useful forms for analysis or presentation.

1.9. Identify, analyze, and compare the institutions, traditions, and art forms of past and present societies.

1.10. Apply acquired information, ideas, and skills to different contexts.

2.1. Plan and make written, oral, and visual presentations for a variety of purposes and audiences.

2.2. Review and revise communications to improve accuracy and clarity.

2.3. Exchange information, questions, and ideas while recognizing the perspectives of others.

2.4. Present perceptions and ideas regarding works of the arts, humanities, and sciences.

2.5. Perform or produce works in the fine and practical arts.

2.7. Use technological tools to exchange information and ideas.

3.1. Identify problems and define their scope and elements.

3.2. Develop and apply strategies based on ways others have prevented or solved problems.

3.3. Develop and apply strategies based on one's own experiences in preventing or solving problems.

3.4. Evaluate the processes used in recognizing and solving problems.

3.5. Reason inductively from a set of specific facts and deductively from general premises.

3.6. Examine problems and proposed solutions from multiple perspectives.

3.7. Evaluate the extent to which a strategy addresses the problem.

3.8. Assess costs, benefits, and other consequences of proposed solutions.

4.1. Explain reasoning and identify information used to support decisions.

4.2. Understand and apply the rights and responsibilities of citizenship in Missouri and in the United States.

4.3. Analyze the duties and responsibilities of individuals in societies.

4.4. Recognize and practice honesty and integrity in academic work.

4.5. Develop, monitor, and revise plans of action to meet deadlines and accomplish those tasks.

Sample Learning Activities

The applicable Show-Me Performance Standards are referenced in parentheses.

* Invite the students to generate questions about immigrants who came to Missouri that interest them. Watch with them "Coming to Missouri: The Immigrant Experience," video no. 7 in the Finding Missouri series. After viewing the video guide them in answering the questions they formulated. (1.1; 1.2; 1.4; 1.5; 2.3)

* Have the students conduct research to find out why so many Germans and Irish left Europe to come to America. Ask them why they think so many of those immigrants chose to settle in Missouri. Explain to them that immigrants have come to America from all parts of the world since the time of first settlement. Discuss the important contributions that immigrants have made and continue to make in the building of America. Remind the students that immigrants continue to come to the United States today. (1.2; 1.9; 2.3)

* Ask the students if they know anyone who came to America from another country. If they do, suggest they interview that person and ask them to tell why she or he came to America. Then have the student report to the class. (1.3; 2.1)

* Read the letter that Jette Bruns wrote to her brother Heinrich. Invite the children to discuss what it would be like to move to a foreign country. What problems do they think they would experience? Have them write a paragraph about "The Problems of Living in a Foreign Country." (1.5; 2.1)

* Have the students locate on a Missouri map these towns with a strong German heritage: Hermann, Westphalia, Washington, Altenberg,

and Wittenberg. Ask if any of them have visited any of these places. If so, they can tell what they saw. (1.3; 1.4)

* Have the students look at the picture of the farm reaper on page 181 and tell how it is different from today's farm machinery. (1.5)

* Have the students conduct research to find out more about the Missouri Botanical Garden in St. Louis. Explore with the students why so many people visit the Missouri Botanical Garden each year. The web site www.mobot.org is a good source of information about Henry Shaw and the various programs and activities that are available. Among other things the students can see pictures of plants that are in bloom at the Missouri Botanical Garden at any given time. Ask the students to draw pictures of some of the plants that they found most interesting. (1.2; 1.4; 1.5; 2.5)

* Discuss with the students the meaning of democracy. Explore with them how democracy has developed in the United States. Ask them to give examples of democratic principles that were in effect in Missouri before the Civil War. Ask them to identify practices from the same period that were not democratic. Discuss whether those undemocratic practices have been changed since then. (1.2; 1.9; 4.2)

* Have the students look at George Caleb Bingham's painting *The County Election*. Discuss how elections were conducted in Missouri before the Civil War. Invite a local election official to visit the class to explain how elections are conducted today. Have the students formulate questions to ask about voting. Conclude the activity by assigning students to draw pictures showing voters today or to make a chart comparing elections and voting in the 1850s with elections and voting today. (1.1; 1.2; 1.3; 1.5; 1.8; 1.9; 2.3; 2.5)

* Ask students to discuss the importance of voting. Have them speculate about why so many people do not vote in elections today. (4.1; 4.2; 4.3)

SUMMARY OF PRINCIPAL POINTS

Missouri grew rapidly during the period between statehood and the Civil War. Its population changed as more settlers from the Northern states and new immigrants from Europe began moving into the state. The Germans and the Irish were the two largest groups of foreign immigrants that came to Missouri. A letter that newly arrived immigrant Henriette Bruns wrote to her brother in Germany is featured in the In Their Own Words section. It depicts some of the difficulties that the new immigrants sometimes encountered. The changing nature of farming and manufacturing and the growth of towns and cities are also examined. The chapter concludes with a discussion of Missouri government and politics. George Caleb Bingham, the frontier painter, is the subject of the Famous Missourian sketch in this chapter.

ANSWERS TO QUESTIONS AND EXERCISES IN THE TEXT

In Their Own Words

1. Answers will vary. Suggested: She was lonesome and probably homesick.

2. Answers will vary. Suggested: She could not easily talk with her American neighbors because she did not speak or understand English well. The workers who were building a new house for her family were very slow in getting it completed. There were problems in operating the farm: a flood destroyed some of their crops, sick horses kept them from plowing the fields properly, they had no place to store the crops after they harvested them, and taking care of her children and doing her housework kept her from planting a big garden.

Testing Yourself

1. Germany.

2. Sausages, sauerbraten, sauerkraut, and stollen.

3. Because of a potato crop failure, many of them were starving in Ireland.

4. Cornmeal, flour, vinegar, rope, lumber, furniture, and tobacco.

5. Because he wanted common people to have more say in their government.

6. The Missouri Botanical Garden.

Things to Talk About

1. Answers will vary. Suggested: different languages; new customs and ways of living; strange climate and surroundings; homesickness.

2. Answers will vary. Suggested: Immigrants provided new workers to help Missouri grow and prosper. They also brought new ideas and ways of doing things, new foods, and new arts and crafts.

3. Women and blacks could not vote. There was no secret ballot. People had to announce their vote out loud. Election day was a special occasion when people got together to talk about politics and to vote. This sometimes led to arguments and quarrels at the polls.

4. Answers will vary.

CHAPTER 10

A DIVIDED COUNTRY

What All Students Should Know

The Guiding Questions listed below are correlated with the text and intended to assist teachers and curriculum designers with the development of unit and lesson plans. The applicable Show-Me Knowledge Standards for Social Studies are referenced in parentheses at the end of each question. A listing of those standards can be found on page 5 of this Guide.

1. How was life different in the Northern states and the Southern states before the Civil War? (SS2; SS4; SS5; SS6)

2. Why did some people want to own slaves? Why did many others believe that it was wrong? (SS6)

3. How did African Americans become slaves? What was life like for slaves? What kinds of work did slaves do? Why weren't they paid for their work? (SS2; SS6; SS7)

4. How did some African American slaves get freedom for themselves? (SS2)

5. How and why did Missourians become involved in the fight over slavery in Kansas? (SS2; SS5)

6. What was the Civil War? How and why did it begin? Why was it one of the most terrible events in American history? (SS2; SS3; SS4; SS5; SS6)

7. How did Abraham Lincoln work to uphold democratic ideals? Why is he considered one of America's greatest presidents? (SS1; SS2; SS3; SS6; SS7)

What All Students Should Be Able to Do

1.1. Develop questions and ideas to initiate and refine research.

1.2. Conduct research to answer questions and evaluate information and ideas.

1.3. Design and conduct field and laboratory investigations to study nature and society.

1.4. Use technological tools and other resources to locate, select, and organize information.

1.5. Comprehend and evaluate written, visual, and oral presentations and works.

1.6. Discover and evaluate patterns and relationships in information.

1.7. Evaluate the accuracy of information and ideas and the reliability of their sources.

1.8. Organize data, information, and ideas into useful forms for analysis or presentation.

1.9. Identify, analyze, and compare the institutions, traditions, and art forms of past and present societies.

1.10. Apply acquired information, ideas, and skills to different contexts.

2.1. Plan and make written, oral, and visual presentations for a variety of purposes and audiences.

2.2. Review and revise communications to improve accuracy and clarity.

2.3. Exchange information, questions, and ideas while recognizing the perspectives of others.

2.4. Present perceptions and ideas regarding works of the arts, humanities, and sciences.

2.5. Perform or produce works in the fine and practical arts.

2.7. Use technological tools to exchange information and ideas.

3.1. Identify problems and define their scope and elements.

3.2. Develop and apply strategies based on ways others have prevented or solved problems.

3.3. Develop and apply strategies based on one's own experiences in preventing or solving problems.

3.4. Evaluate the processes used in recognizing and solving problems.

3.5. Reason inductively from a set of specific facts and deductively from general premises.

3.6. Examine problems and proposed solutions from multiple perspectives.

3.7. Evaluate the extent to which a strategy addresses the problem.

3.8. Assess costs, benefits, and other consequences of proposed solutions.

4.1. Explain reasoning and identify information used to support decisions.

4.2. Understand and apply the rights and responsibilities of citizenship in Missouri and in the United States.

4.3. Analyze the duties and responsibilities of individuals in societies.

4.4. Recognize and practice honesty and integrity in academic work.

4.5. Develop, monitor, and revise plans of action to meet deadlines and accomplish those tasks.

Sample Learning Activities

The applicable Show-Me Performance Standards are referenced in parentheses.

* Discuss the differences between the North and the South that are mentioned in this text. Make a chart showing these differences. Ask the students to speculate about what might have happened in the South during this period if the cotton crop had been ruined one year by flood, drought, or insects. Ask them if they believe that the same thing would have happened to the North if the wheat crop there had failed. Have them justify their conclusion. (1.2; 1.5; 1.6; 1.8)

* Give the students an outline map of the United States. Have them label and color with one color all of the states that were free states in 1860. Have them label and color with another color all of the states that were slave states in 1860. (1.4; 1.9)

* Have the students conduct research about slave life. Have them look at the various illustrations in this chapter to see what they can discover about how slaves were treated. Ask them to tell what the sheriff's sale bill on page 200 and the newspaper reward notice on page 201 say about the treatment of slaves. Have the students write a paragraph on why they would not want to be a slave. (1.2; 1.5; 1.6; 2.1)

* Discuss how slaves felt about their treatment. Ask them to describe the different ways that slaves attempted to gain freedom for themselves and their families. Ask them to compare the experiences of John Berry Meachum, William Wells Brown, Harriet and Dred Scott, Hiram Young, and James P. Beckwourth. Create a Hall of Fame display featuring the accomplishments of these famous Missouri African Americans who had once been slaves. (1.2; 1.6; 2.1)

* View with the students "What Do We Stand For?" video no. 10 in the Finding Missouri series. Use it to introduce students to the Dred Scott case. After watching the video ask them to decide how they would have voted if they had been on the jury. (1.4; 1.5; 4.2)

* Ask the students to consider why people treat each other the way they do. What happens when people treat others kindly? What happens when they treat them unkindly? Why do they think that some people owned slaves and others believed that it was wrong to own slaves? (2.3; 3.1; 4.3)

* Assign the students to do research to learn more about Abraham Lincoln. What unique qualities did Abraham Lincoln possess? What made his life story so remarkable? What important things did he accomplish? Ask them to summarize their findings by writing a paragraph about "Abraham Lincoln: A Great American." (1.2; 1.5; 1.8; 2.1).

* Discuss with the students why Abraham Lincoln was so determined not to allow the breakup of the United States. Explain to them that Lincoln believed that the Civil War was a struggle to preserve democracy in America. In the Gettysburg Address he called upon Americans to honor those who had died in the Civil War by resolving to ensure that "government of the people, by the people, and for the people should not perish from the earth." (1.9; 4.2)

SUMMARY OF PRINCIPAL POINTS

This chapter describes the basic differences between the Northern states and the Southern states. Slavery and slave life are discussed. The story of William Wells Brown, a Missouri slave who escaped to freedom, tells much about being a slave. So does the featured document, a sheriff's sale handbill offering African American slaves in Boone County for sale along with animals. Dred and Harriet

Scott's attempts to win their freedom in court focused more attention on the slavery issue and made them famous. Special attention is given to the role of the free blacks and their many accomplishments and contributions. The debate over whether slavery should be allowed in the new lands to the west led to conflict along the Missouri-Kansas border. This and other important disagreements contributed to a split between the North and the South. When Northerner Abraham Lincoln was elected president in 1860, some of the Southern states left the Union and formed a separate country. Lincoln refused to allow them to leave the United States, and the Civil War began. St. Louis businessman and preacher John Berry Meachum is profiled as the Famous Missourian.

ANSWERS TO QUESTIONS AND EXCERCISES IN THE TEXT

In Their Own Words
1. Columbia, Missouri.
2. Slaves and livestock.
3. When people could not pay their debts the court ordered the sheriff to take their property and sell it to pay off those debts. Missouri laws said that slaves were property.
4. Answers will vary.
5. Answers will vary. Suggested: Slaves were sometimes treated no better than animals. They had few legal rights. Even young children could be sold.

Testing Yourself
1. South.
2. North.
3. Cotton.
4. North.
5. Jeanette Fourchet, John Berry Meachum, Hiram Young, and Jim Beckwourth.
6. Because many people were killed or wounded there while fighting over slavery.
7. The leaders of those states did not like Lincoln's ideas about slavery. They also thought that the North had taken over the national government.

Things to Talk About
1. More people lived in the North. The North had more cities, factories, and businesses. Most Northern farmers lived on small farms and raised many kinds of products. There were few slaves in the North. Most people in the South lived on small farms, but there were some very large farms called plantations. They used slaves to do most of the work on plantations. Cotton was the main crop in the South. The Southern economy depended almost entirely on agriculture.
2. Answers will vary. Suggested: the slaves received no pay for their work. They

were not allowed to make any choices for themselves. They were often not allowed to marry or to go to school. They could be sold and taken away from their families. Cruel masters sometimes treated them harshly. No person has a right to own another person.

3. He left the country because he was afraid that if he stayed in the United States he might be arrested and sent back to his owner in Missouri.

4. Answers will vary.

True or False

1. False. Cotton was grown on plantations in the South.

2. False. Slaves were not paid for their work.

3. True.

4. True.

5. False. Free blacks had fewer rights than white people.

6. False. Abolitionists were against slavery.

7. False. Very few people in the South voted for Abraham Lincoln for president.

CHAPTER 11

THE CIVIL WAR COMES TO MISSOURI

What All Students Should Know

The Guiding Questions listed below are correlated with the text and are intended to assist teachers and curriculum designers with the development of unit and lesson plans. The applicable Show-Me Knowledge Standards for Social Studies are referenced in parentheses at the end of each question. A listing of those standards can be found on page 5 of this Guide.

1. Why were Missourians divided over which side to support in the Civil War? (SS2; SS4; SS5; SS6)

2. Why is a civil war an especially terrible kind of war? (SS6)

3. What were some important battles fought in Missouri during the Civil War? (SS2)

4. In what ways was the Civil War in Missouri different from the war in other parts of the country? (SS2; SS6)

5. How did the Civil War affect the lives of families, women, children, and African Americans in Missouri? (SS2; SS6)

6. What changes resulted from the Civil War? (SS2)

What All Students Should Be Able to Do

1.1. Develop questions and ideas to initiate and refine research.

1.2. Conduct research to answer questions and evaluate information and ideas.

1.3. Design and conduct field and laboratory investigations to study nature and society.

1.4. Use technological tools and other resources to locate, select, and organize information.

1.5. Comprehend and evaluate written, visual, and oral presentations and works.

1.6. Discover and evaluate patterns and relationships in information.

1.7. Evaluate the accuracy of information and ideas and the reliability of their sources.

1.8. Organize data, information, and ideas into useful forms for analysis or presentation.

1.9. Identify, analyze, and compare the institutions, traditions, and art forms of past and present societies.

1.10. Apply acquired information, ideas, and skills to different contexts.

2.1. Plan and make written, oral, and visual presentations for a variety of purposes and audiences.

2.2. Review and revise communications to improve accuracy and clarity.

2.3. Exchange information, questions, and ideas while recognizing the perspectives of others.

2.4. Present perceptions and ideas regarding works of the arts, humanities, and sciences.

2.5. Perform or produce works in the fine and practical arts.

2.7. Use technological tools to exchange information and ideas.

3.1. Identify problems and define their scope and elements.

3.2. Develop and apply strategies based on ways others have prevented or solved problems.

3.3. Develop and apply strategies based on one's own experiences in preventing or solving problems.

3.4. Evaluate the processes used in recognizing and solving problems.

3.5. Reason inductively from a set of specific facts and deductively from general premises.

3.6. Examine problems and proposed solutions from multiple perspectives.

3.7. Evaluate the extent to which a strategy addresses the problem.

3.8. Assess costs, benefits, and other consequences of proposed solutions.

4.1. Explain reasoning and identify information used to support decisions.

4.2. Understand and apply the rights and responsibilities of citizenship in Missouri and in the United States.

4.3. Analyze the duties and responsibilities of individuals in societies.

4.4. Recognize and practice honesty and integrity in academic work.

4.5. Develop, monitor, and revise plans of action to meet deadlines and accomplish those tasks.

Sample Learning Activities

The applicable Show-Me Performance Standards are referenced in parentheses.

* Have the students suggest different things that might have caused someone to support a particular side during the Civil War. Invite them to speculate about why choosing sides would have been more difficult for some people than for others. Ask them to identify groups that would have been more likely to support the North. Which ones would have been more likely to support the South? (1.1; 1.2; 1.5; 3.6)

* Divide the class into groups. Assign each group to conduct research to learn more about a different Civil War battle in Missouri. Have them write a newspaper story about the battle. Remind them to answer such questions as who, what, when, where, why, and how. Have each group report its findings to the other members of the class. The students could then compare how the different battles they studied were alike and different. (1.2; 2.1; 2.3)

* Have the students conduct research to find out what Civil War battles or skirmishes may have been fought in their locality. If possible arrange for them to visit a local historical society or museum to find out more about their community during the Civil War. Perhaps there are some letters, newspaper stories, memoirs, local histories, or other kinds of sources for them to examine. You could use this as an opportunity to talk about how to determine the reliability of different kinds of sources. When the research is completed the students might prepare a booklet about the Civil War in their community using stories, pictures, maps, and any other materials they have found. (1.2; 1.3; 1.7; 2.1)

* Invite a Civil War reenactor to come to the class in costume to talk with the students about the Civil War and about historical reenactment. Have the students formulate questions to ask about the Civil War. (1.1; 1.3; 2.3)

* Have students find songs that were popular during the Civil War. If recordings are available listen to them and solicit student reactions to them. (1.9; 2.4)

* Have the students examine George Caleb Bingham's painting *Order Number Eleven* shown on page 223. Ask them to write a paragraph describing the things that they see in this painting and what they believe that Bingham was trying to say about the Civil War in Missouri. (1.9; 2.1; 2.4)

* Read Amos Camden Riley's letters to his parents. Invite the students to respond to the questions on page 228. Assign the students to see if they can find copies of other letters that were written during the Civil War. The *Missouri Historical Review* has through the years published many Civil War letters and journals written by Missourians. Most Missouri public libraries have copies of the *Missouri Historical Review* in their collections. Ask the students to compare how the letters are alike and different. (1.2; 1.5; 1.7; 2.1)

* Have each student pretend that he or she was a soldier or a nurse during the Civil War. Ask them to write a letter to their parents telling them about their experiences. (1.2; 2.1)

* Discuss with the students how the Civil War affected African Americans in Missouri. Dramatize Archer Alexander's first meeting with William Greenleaf Eliot. (1.5; 2.1; 2.5)

SUMMARY OF PRINCIPAL POINTS

Missouri is shown to be a border state whose people were divided on the question of staying in the Union or joining the Confederate States of America. The state did not leave the Union, but many Missourians chose to fight for the South anyway. Major battles and military campaigns in Missouri are mentioned. Attention is also given to guerrilla warfare and how the war affected African Americans and women. The students can read portions of two letters that Colonel Amos Camden Riley wrote to his parents while he was away from home fighting in the Civil War.

ADDITIONAL INFORMATION

The Civil War is sometimes portrayed as a glamorous or even romantic struggle. Remind your students that it was a long and bloody war in which many people were killed. More than six hundred thousand Americans lost their lives in the Civil War. That number is about equal to the total number of Americans killed in all of the United States' other wars combined, including the Revolutionary War, the War of 1812, the Mexican War, the Spanish-American War, World War I, World War II, and the wars in Korea and Vietnam.

The population of the United States in 1860 was only a little more than thirty-one million. This meant that almost one out of every fifty Americans was killed in the war. Many more were injured and wounded. Few American families escaped having one of their members either killed or wounded.

ANSWERS TO QUESTIONS AND EXERCISES IN THE TEXT

In Their Own Words
1. Getting news from home and asking about family members and things on

the farm; describing health conditions in army camps; reassuring his family that he was OK and not sad or depressed; that he needed some clothes; and the death of his friend.

2. Homesickness, illnesses, and bad conditions in army camps; traveling from place to place; shortages of supplies; fighting in battles and the dangers of injury or death.

3. Answers will vary. In both letters Riley said he wanted to hear news from home and he told his family that he was well. By the time he wrote his second letter, he had been fighting in battles and had seen people die from disease and from the fighting.

4. His friend had died and he had seen people killed in battle. There was no sign that the war would end soon.

Testing Yourself
1. Francis P. Blair, Jr.

2. Yes, Missouri stayed in the Union, but some Missourians supported the Confederate States of America and took part in its government.

3. They rolled hemp bales in front of them to protect themselves from Union bullets.

4. They often hid out in the bushes and the woods; they attacked enemy towns and property and then rode away.

5. To St. Louis, a Union army camp, or a free state. They were seeking freedom, and some of them wanted to fight for the Union.

6. Answers may vary. Suggested: the North and South were reunited; slavery was ended.

Fill in the Blanks
1. Abraham Lincoln.
2. Confederate States of America.
3. Union.
4. blue.
5. gray.
6. Union.
7. border.
8. North, or Union.

Things to Talk About
1. Lincoln did not own slaves because he did not like slavery and because he lived in the North.

2. Because they believed that they would be freed if the Union won.

3. They were guerrillas who killed and robbed Union supporters during the Civil War. They supported the South, but they were not regular soldiers in the Confederate army.

4. Many women volunteered to work in hospitals to help care for wounded soldiers and to do their part for the war effort. This also gave them new opportunities to work outside of the home, and it allowed those who were hired as nurses to earn money.

5. Answers will vary.

6. Because the people who are fighting each other live in the same country. That means that neighbors and family members are sometimes on opposite sides in the conflict.

CHAPTER 12
RECONSTRUCTION IN MISSOURI

What All Students Should Know

The Guiding Questions listed below are correlated with the text and intended to assist teachers and curriculum designers with the development of unit and lesson plans. The applicable Show-Me Knowledge Standards for Social Studies are referenced in parentheses at the end of each question. A listing of those standards can be found on page 5 of this Guide.

1. What problems did Americans face after the Civil War? How did government leaders attempt to solve those problems? (SS2; SS3)

2. How was life different for African Americans following the war? What problems did former slaves face? (SS2; SS6)

3. How were railroads an improvement over earlier forms of transportation? What kinds of changes did the expansion of railroads bring to Missouri after the Civil War? (SS2; SS4; SS5; SS7)

4. Why did some people find it so difficult to make peace after the war? (SS6)

What All Students Should Be Able to Do

1.1. Develop questions and ideas to initiate and refine research.

1.2. Conduct research to answer questions and evaluate information and ideas.

1.3. Design and conduct field and laboratory investigations to study nature and society.

1.4. Use technological tools and other resources to locate, select, and organize information.

1.5. Comprehend and evaluate written, visual, and oral presentations and works.

1.6. Discover and evaluate patterns and relationships in information.

1.7. Evaluate the accuracy of information and ideas and the reliability of their sources.

1.8. Organize data, information, and ideas into useful forms for analysis or presentation.

1.9. Identify, analyze, and compare the institutions, traditions, and art forms of past and present societies.

1.10. Apply acquired information, ideas, and skills to different contexts.

2.1. Plan and make written, oral, and visual presentations for a variety of purposes and audiences.

2.2. Review and revise communications to improve accuracy and clarity.

2.3. Exchange information, questions, and ideas while recognizing the perspectives of others.

2.4. Present perceptions and ideas regarding works of the arts, humanities, and sciences.

2.5. Perform or produce works in the fine and practical arts.

2.7. Use technological tools to exchange information and ideas.

3.1. Identify problems and define their scope and elements.

3.2. Develop and apply strategies based on ways others have prevented or solved problems.

3.3. Develop and apply strategies based on one's own experiences in preventing or solving problems.

3.4. Evaluate the processes used in recognizing and solving problems.

3.5. Reason inductively from a set of specific facts and deductively from general premises.

3.6. Examine problems and proposed solutions from multiple perspectives.

3.7. Evaluate the extent to which a strategy addresses the problem.

3.8. Assess costs, benefits, and other consequences of proposed solutions.

4.1. Explain reasoning and identify information used to support decisions.

4.2. Understand and apply the rights and responsibilities of citizenship in Missouri and in the United States.

4.3. Analyze the duties and responsibilities of individuals in societies.

4.4. Recognize and practice honesty and integrity in academic work.

4.5. Develop, monitor, and revise plans of action to meet deadlines and accomplish those tasks.

Sample Learning Activities

The applicable Show-Me Performance Standards are referenced in parentheses.

* Ask the students to discuss how winners should treat losers following a sporting contest. Have them decide if they think that it would be more difficult for winners in a war to treat members of the losing side kindly. After the Civil War why did some people in Missouri want to punish anyone who had supported the South in that contest? Do they believe that Lincoln was right to be more interested in restoring peace than in punishing the South? (1.6; 2.3; 3.1; 4.1)

* Conduct a discussion about why it was so important to establish schools for African Americans following the Civil War. Have students do research to identify individuals and groups who worked to create black schools in Missouri during the postwar period. Remind students that the schools for black children were separate from the schools for white children. (1.2; 1.5; 2.3)

* Assign the students to conduct research to find out when the first railroads reached their area. Also ask them to investigate how the construction of railroads changed their city or town. Assist them in summarizing their findings and have each student write a paragraph "How the railroads changed our community." (1.2; 1.6; 1.8; 2.1)

* Have the students tell if they believe railroads are still important today. Have them decide if they have become less important than they once were. Why? (1.6)

* Give each student a copy of the chart below showing the total number of miles of railroad tracks in Missouri.

TOTAL NUMBER OF MILES OF RAILROAD TRACKS IN MISSOURI BY DECADE

Year	Total number of miles of railroad tracks in Missouri.
1850	0 miles
1860	810 miles
1870	2,000 miles
1880	4,000 miles
1890	6,100 miles
1900	6,900 miles

Assign them to make a bar graph showing the Number of Miles of Railroad Track in Missouri. Show the miles along the left margin and the years along the bottom margin. After they have completed their graphs, ask the students to determine during which ten-year period the most new railroad tracks were laid in Missouri. (1.6; 1.8)

* View with the students the segment on the Eads Bridge in "Growth of Cities," video no. 13 in the Finding Missouri series. Ask the students

to identify some problems James Eads had to overcome in order to build a bridge across the Mississippi River. Discuss why the development of railroads made construction of a bridge across the Mississippi necessary. Have the students make a list of any technological innovations he used in building his bridge. Ask the students to draw a picture of the Eads Bridge or perhaps someone would like to construct a model of the bridge. (1.2; 1.4; 1.6; 2.1; 2.5)

* Ask the students to discuss why Jesse and Frank James are so famous. After the Civil War, why did some people try to make them heroes? Have the class decide if the argument that members of the James gang were like Robin Hood is fact or myth. What evidence do they have to support their conclusion? (1.6; 1.7)

SUMMARY OF PRINCIPAL POINTS

During Reconstruction, Missourians quickly restored or rebuilt the property damaged by the war, and the state continued to grow and to prosper. The expansion of railroads throughout the state accelerated economic development in postwar Missouri. Healing the ill will generated among Missourians by the war was not so easily accomplished. By 1875 the state had removed the legal restrictions from former Confederate sympathizers, and all white male Missourians had regained their full civil rights. The struggle to win equal rights for Missouri blacks was less successful. Although blacks were better off than they had been as slaves and many individual blacks achieved great successes in their chosen fields, blacks were still treated as second-class citizens. The story of Charles and Bettie Birthright offers an example of former slaves who overcame many of the obstacles African Americans faced. Women also sought more rights, especially the right to vote, but their efforts failed to accomplish that goal. Missouri also gained the dubious distinction of being called the Outlaw State when former bushwhackers such as Jesse and Frank James continued their violent ways as killers and bank robbers. Governor Thomas T. Crittenden's proclamation offering a substantial reward for the arrest and capture of some of the state's most notorious outlaws reprinted in this chapter allows students to learn about their misdeeds. James Milton Turner, an African American educator and diplomat, is the featured Famous Missourian.

ANSWERS TO QUESTIONS AND EXERCISES IN THE TEXT

In Their Own Words
1. Robbery and murder.
2. To steal the money, valuable packages, and mail that the train carried.
3. Jesse and Frank James.
4. $5,000 for their arrest and another $5,000 for the conviction of either of the James brothers.

5. Because the governor wanted to end the killings and robberies and also because many people believed that these outlaws were giving the state a bad name.

Testing Yourself

1. The people of Missouri had been badly divided. Each side blamed the other for causing the war. The two sides had to learn to live together again. Now that the slaves finally had gained their freedom, they had to start new lives for themselves. They wanted to have the same rights as white Missourians. The buildings and property that had been destroyed by the war also had to be rebuilt.

2. Lincoln was shot and killed by John Wilkes Booth, an angry actor who had supported the South.

3. The slaves were freed, many school buildings were built, the state started new schools for black children and to train teachers, businesses were reopened, and many new railroads were built.

4. Frank P. Blair, Jr.

5. They worked hard to provide for their families. They also attempted to win the right to vote. They helped start schools for their children. They also organized and ran their own churches.

6. African Americans and women.

Choose the Right Words

1. less.
2. came to.
3. Confederate.
4. United States senators.

Things to Talk About

1. Railroads were built in all parts of the state. They were faster, could carry heavier loads, and were more comfortable for passengers. Engineers built new and better bridges that made it easier to cross rivers when traveling.

2. Answers will vary.

3. People who had supported the Confederate guerrillas and had wanted the South to win the Civil War accused the Union side of picking on the James boys. They compared Jesse James to Robin Hood, whom they said robbed the rich and gave to the poor.

CHAPTER 13
CHANGING TIMES IN MISSOURI

What All Students Should Know

The Guiding Questions listed below are correlated with the text and intended to assist teachers and curriculum designers with the development of unit and lesson plans. The applicable Show-Me Knowledge Standards for Social Studies are referenced in parentheses at the end of each question. A listing of those standards can be found on page 5 of this Guide.

1. In the years between the end of the Civil War (1865) and the beginning of World War I (1914) how was life in Missouri changing? How did improvements in technology and new inventions contribute to those changes? (SS2)

2. What examples of those changes might a visitor to the 1904 St. Louis World's Fair have seen? (SS2)

3. How did these changes affect farmers, factory workers, and women? (SS6)

4. What new scientific discoveries made George Washington Carver famous? (SS2)

What All Students Should Be Able to Do

1.1. Develop questions and ideas to initiate and refine research.

1.2. Conduct research to answer questions and evaluate information and ideas.

1.3. Design and conduct field and laboratory investigations to study nature and society.

1.4. Use technological tools and other resources to locate, select, and organize information.

1.5. Comprehend and evaluate written, visual, and oral presentations and works.

1.6. Discover and evaluate patterns and relationships in information.

1.7. Evaluate the accuracy of information and ideas and the reliability of their sources.

1.8. Organize data, information, and ideas into useful forms for analysis or presentation.

1.9. Identify, analyze, and compare the institutions, traditions, and art forms of past and present societies.

1.10. Apply acquired information, ideas, and skills to different contexts.

2.1. Plan and make written, oral, and visual presentations for a variety of purposes and audiences.

2.2. Review and revise communications to improve accuracy and clarity.

2.3. Exchange information, questions, and ideas while recognizing the perspectives of others.

2.4. Present perceptions and ideas regarding works of the arts, humanities, and sciences.

2.5. Perform or produce works in the fine and practical arts.

2.7. Use technological tools to exchange information and ideas.

3.1. Identify problems and define their scope and elements.

3.2. Develop and apply strategies based on ways others have prevented or solved problems.

3.3. Develop and apply strategies based on one's own experiences in preventing or solving problems.

3.4. Evaluate the processes used in recognizing and solving problems.

3.5. Reason inductively from a set of specific facts and deductively from general premises.

3.6. Examine problems and proposed solutions from multiple perspectives.

3.7. Evaluate the extent to which a strategy addresses the problem.

3.8. Assess costs, benefits, and other consequences of proposed solutions.

4.1. Explain reasoning and identify information used to support decisions.

4.2. Understand and apply the rights and responsibilities of citizenship in Missouri and in the United States.

4.3. Analyze the duties and responsibilities of individuals in societies.

4.4. Recognize and practice honesty and integrity in academic work.

4.5. Develop, monitor, and revise plans of action to meet deadlines and accomplish those tasks.

Sample Learning Activities

The applicable Show-Me Performance Standards are referenced in parentheses.

* You might introduce this unit by viewing with the class "Come to the Fair," video no. 14 in the Finding Missouri series. Invite the children to describe some of the things that they could have seen at the St. Louis World's Fair. Ask them to identify which of those things were examples of advances in technology. (1.4; 1.5; 1.6)

* Use the Think/Pair/Share cooperative learning structure to ask students to decide how they might have traveled to the St. Louis World's Fair in 1904. How would they travel to St. Louis today? (1.2; 1.9)

* Have each student pretend that they had visited the St. Louis

67

World's Fair. Assign them to write a letter to a friend describing some of the things that they had seen and done. (1.5; 2.1)

* Ask the students to make a list of the new inventions that were made during this period. Discuss with them how each of these inventions would have changed the way people lived. (1.2; 1.5)

* Have the students bring pictures and models of early cars. Let them discuss some of the differences between those cars and today's models. Learning the names of the old cars might be fun for the pupils. For a class display, put the pictures or models in order according to the dates when they were made. (1.9; 2.1)

* Have the students conduct research to find out more about George Washington Carver and his discoveries. Have them draw pictures of some of the agricultural products that he experimented with and the uses he made with them. (1.2; 2.1)

* Discuss what new jobs were opened to women during this period. How did these new opportunities for employment outside of the home change things for women and girls? (1.2; 1.9; 3.1)

* The students might enjoy setting up a model general store. They could bring from home small quantities of unpackaged food items, small pieces of cloth, doll clothes, toy tools, and so on, and arrange them in a model store. (2.1)

* Have the students look at the picture of the 1890 University of Missouri football team. Ask them to describe how the uniforms and ball are different from those used in that sport today. How do they think that a football game in 1890 might have been different from a football game today? (1.9)

SUMMARY OF PRINCIPAL POINTS

The years between the end of the Civil War (1865) and the beginning of World War I (1914) produced great changes in the United States and Missouri. The Louisiana Purchase Exposition of 1904 displayed, in an exciting way, many of the social and technological changes that were transforming America.

This chapter describes the coming of the automobile and the opening of telephone service. It traces the growth of cities, and it shows how the factory system began to make use of new and complex machinery, produce more goods, make life easier and more pleasant, and alter the way many Missourians worked. Urban workers in factories faced new problems. Farmers moved from pioneer farming techniques to modern agricultural methods with the help of new types of farm equipment and new farming techniques. Country general stores and urban department stores were important mercantile establishments. Women's roles were also undergoing change as more women held full-time jobs outside of the home. Susan Blow, a teacher who helped establish kindergartens in the United States, is featured as the Famous Missourian. A sketch of George Washington Carver examines his scientific accomplishments.

ANSWERS TO QUESTIONS AND EXERCISES IN THE TEXT

Things to Do
1. Telephones, electric lights, washing machines, electric irons, phonographs, vacuum cleaners, hot and cold running water, indoor toilets, box cameras, and automobiles.
2. Scenes will vary.
3. Letters will vary.

Things to Talk About
1. To find jobs and work in new factories. Some also were attracted by the excitement of city life.
2. George Washington Carver overcame great odds to become a famous teacher and scientist. He was best known for important research about peanuts, sweet potatoes, and other foods. Carter also worked to improve relations between the races.
3. Because they were powered by an engine and not by horses.

Fill in the Blank
1. Thomas Edison.
2. Louisiana Purchase.
3. "Meet Me in Saint Louis."
4. railroad, automobiles.
5. Tom Bass.
6. James Eads.
7. labor unions.
8. Kansas City and St. Joseph.
9. National League.

CHAPTER 14

SOME GOOD TIMES AND BAD TIMES

What All Students Should Know

The Guiding Questions listed below are correlated with the text and are intended to assist teachers and curriculum designers with the development of unit and lesson plans. The applicable Show-Me Knowledge Standards for Social Studies are referenced in parentheses at the end of each question. A listing of those standards can be found on page 5 of this Guide.

1. Why did many Missourians not want America to get involved in World War I? What changed their minds? When the United States did join the war, what roles did Missourians play in making a victory possible? (SS2; SS3; SS5; SS6)

2. What new forms of transportation were changing the way people traveled during this period? (SS2; SS5)

3. Why was the decision to give women the right to vote such an important development in the history of the United States? (SS1; SS2; SS3; SS6)

4. What is a depression? What kinds of things cause depressions? How do depressions affect people's lives? How did government attempt to make conditions better for Americans during the Great Depression? (SS2; SS3; SS4)

What All Students Should Be Able to Do

1.1. Develop questions and ideas to initiate and refine research.

1.2. Conduct research to answer questions and evaluate information and ideas.

1.3. Design and conduct field and laboratory investigations to study nature and society.

1.4. Use technological tools and other resources to locate, select, and organize information.

1.5. Comprehend and evaluate written, visual, and oral presentations and works.

1.6. Discover and evaluate patterns and relationships in information.

1.7. Evaluate the accuracy of information and ideas and the reliability of their sources.

1.8. Organize data, information, and ideas into useful forms for analysis or presentation.

1.9. Identify, analyze, and compare the institutions, traditions, and art forms of past and present societies.

1.10. Apply acquired information, ideas, and skills to different contexts.

2.1. Plan and make written, oral, and visual presentations for a variety of purposes and audiences.

2.2. Review and revise communications to improve accuracy and clarity.

2.3. Exchange information, questions, and ideas while recognizing the perspectives of others.

2.4. Present perceptions and ideas regarding works of the arts, humanities, and sciences.

2.5. Perform or produce works in the fine and practical arts.

2.7. Use technological tools to exchange information and ideas.

3.1. Identify problems and define their scope and elements.

3.2. Develop and apply strategies based on ways others have prevented or solved problems.

3.3. Develop and apply strategies based on one's own experiences in preventing or solving problems.

3.4. Evaluate the processes used in recognizing and solving problems.

3.5. Reason inductively from a set of specific facts and deductively from general premises.

3.6. Examine problems and proposed solutions from multiple perspectives.

3.7. Evaluate the extent to which a strategy addresses the problem.

3.8. Assess costs, benefits, and other consequences of proposed solutions.

4.1. Explain reasoning and identify information used to support decisions.

4.2. Understand and apply the rights and responsibilities of citizenship in Missouri and in the United States.

4.3. Analyze the duties and responsibilities of individuals in societies.

4.4. Recognize and practice honesty and integrity in academic work.

4.5. Develop, monitor, and revise plans of action to meet deadlines and accomplish those tasks.

Sample Learning Activities

The applicable Show-Me Performance Standards are referenced in parentheses.

* Refer the students to the map on page 311. Help them locate the Central Powers and the Allies. (1.4)

* Talk about why the American people felt so far from the war in Europe and thought that they did not need to get involved in it. During the discussion, it might be helpful to mention that in 1917 no person had yet flown across the Atlantic Ocean in an airplane and that it usually took the fastest ships about a week to cross the Atlantic. (1.5; 2.1; 2.3)

* Discuss with the students why Americans consider automobiles so important. Ask them how the size of the United States increases America's reliance on automobile transportation. Invite them to consider why in the future Americans might have to rely more on mass transportation systems. Ask the students to write a paragraph about "How the Automobile Changed America," or "Why Americans Love Their Cars." (1.5; 2.1; 3.1)

* Assign the students to conduct research to learn more about the campaign by women to win the right to vote. Discuss how this change was another step in building democracy in America. (1.2; 4.2)

* Invite the students to do research to identify some government programs that were established during the Great Depression to make life better for Americans. Mention things such as Social Security, programs to provide aid to farmers, insurance for bank deposits. Use this as an opportunity to discuss how government decisions affect people. Ask them to identify some government programs that are being discussed today. (1.2; 2.3; 3.1; 3.2; 4.3)

* Explain to the class that today there are many more laws governing the ways banks and savings associations are run than there were in the 1930s. Now each person's savings are insured up to a certain amount, and, if the bank closes, the United States government will repay the money up to that amount. Because there was no federal bank insurance in the thirties, many people lost their money. (1.2; 2.1; 3.2)

SUMMARY OF PRINCIPAL POINTS

This chapter covers the varied and changing scene in Missouri from the outbreak of World War I in Europe to just before the beginning of World War II. When fighting first erupted in Europe in 1914, the United States tried to remain neutral, but events such as the German U-boat attacks caused the United States to enter World War I in 1917. World War I was followed by a period of prosperity that ended with an economic crash in 1929. The social and economic conditions in Missouri during World War I, the 1920s, and the Great Depression are discussed with special attention being given to the "new woman" and African Americans. The experiences of a family from northeast Missouri will help students understand what life was like during the depression. General John J. Pershing is the Famous Missourian featured in this chapter.

ANSWERS TO QUESTIONS AND EXERCISES IN THE TEXT

Testing Yourself

1. The Germans began using U-boats to sink unarmed ships without warning.

2. Many Missourians joined the army or the navy and fought in Europe. Some Missouri women volunteered to work in Red Cross canteens in America and Europe. Missouri farmers raised more food to help feed the armies in Europe. Families tried not to waste anything. Workers in Missouri's factories produced clothing, shoes, chemicals, weapons, and many other things needed to fight the war. Missourians also bought war bonds to help pay for the war.

3. Radio and motion pictures.

4. He was the first person to fly an airplane across the Atlantic Ocean alone.

5. Business was bad; factories closed; people lost their jobs and their homes; banks closed; families did not have enough money to buy food.

6. People were hired by the government to repair and build new roads, to make

new parks and playgrounds, to build new buildings, to construct dams, and to plant trees.

7. Women.

8. Gaines asked the courts to allow African Americans to attend the University of Missouri.

Things to Talk About

1. Answers will vary.

2. Answers will vary.

3. They went to movies, listened to radio programs, attended dances and listened to music, and watched sporting events.

4. Paige was a great pitcher, but because of segregation the major league baseball teams would not allow an African American to play for them. That did not change until 1947, which was near the end of Paige's baseball career.

Matching Partners

1-d; 2-a; 3-b; 4-e; 5-c

Choose the Right Words

1. Allies.

2. Central Powers.

3. U-boats.

4. automobile.

CHAPTER 15

MISSOURIANS JOIN STRUGGLES IN FARAWAY PLACES AND AT HOME

What All Students Should Know

The Guiding Questions listed below are correlated with the text and intended to assist teachers and curriculum designers with the development of unit and lesson plans. The applicable Show-Me Knowledge Standards for Social Studies are referenced in parentheses at the end of each question. A listing of those standards can be found on page 5 of this Guide.

1. Why do countries fight wars? Why did the United States decide to fight in World War II? What were they fighting for? How was the defeat of the Axis Powers a victory for democratic ideals? (SS1; SS2; SS3; SS5; SS7)

2. What contributions did Missourians make during World War II? (SS2; SS6; SS7)

3. What makes people famous? Why is Harry Truman one of the most famous Missourians of all time? (SS2; SS6; SS7)

4. How did the Civil Rights and Women's Rights movements contribute to the fulfillment of democratic ideals? (SS1; SS2; SS6)

What All Students Should Be Able to Do

1.1. Develop questions and ideas to initiate and refine research.

1.2. Conduct research to answer questions and evaluate information and ideas.

1.3. Design and conduct field and laboratory investigations to study nature and society.

1.4. Use technological tools and other resources to locate, select, and organize information.

1.5. Comprehend and evaluate written, visual, and oral presentations and works.

1.6. Discover and evaluate patterns and relationships in information.

1.7. Evaluate the accuracy of information and ideas and the reliability of their sources.

1.8. Organize data, information, and ideas into useful forms for analysis or presentation.

1.9. Identify, analyze, and compare the institutions, traditions, and art forms of past and present societies.

1.10. Apply acquired information, ideas, and skills to different contexts.

2.1. Plan and make written, oral, and visual presentations for a variety of purposes and audiences.

2.2. Review and revise communications to improve accuracy and clarity.

2.3. Exchange information, questions, and ideas while recognizing the perspectives of others.

2.4. Present perceptions and ideas regarding works of the arts, humanities, and sciences.

2.5. Perform or produce works in the fine and practical arts.

2.7. Use technological tools to exchange information and ideas.

3.1. Identify problems and define their scope and elements.

3.2. Develop and apply strategies based on ways others have prevented or solved problems.

3.3. Develop and apply strategies based on one's own experiences in preventing or solving problems.

3.4. Evaluate the processes used in recognizing and solving problems.

3.5. Reason inductively from a set of specific facts and deductively from general premises.

3.6. Examine problems and proposed solutions from multiple perspectives.

3.7. Evaluate the extent to which a strategy addresses the problem.

3.8. Assess costs, benefits, and other consequences of proposed solutions.

4.1. Explain reasoning and identify information used to support decisions.

4.2. Understand and apply the rights and responsibilities of citizenship in Missouri and in the United States.

4.3. Analyze the duties and responsibilities of individuals in societies.

4.4. Recognize and practice honesty and integrity in academic work.

4.5. Develop, monitor, and revise plans of action to meet deadlines and accomplish those tasks.

Sample Learning Activities

The applicable Show-Me Performance Standards are referenced in parentheses.

* Have the students conduct research to learn more about Adolf Hitler and the attack on Pearl Harbor and how they influenced America's decision to enter World War II. (1.2; 1.5; 1.6)

* Ask the students to conduct research to find out how children contributed to the war effort. Have them discuss what responsibilities children have as citizens. Ask them to identify things children can do today to make America and the world a better place. (1.2; 1.10; 2.3; 3.2; 4.2; 4.3)

* Read Governor Donnell's proclamation. Ask them if they believe that recycling is necessary only during wartime. Have them discuss the benefits of recycling and conservation. Ask them to identify ways that they might participate in conservation and recycling programs. (1.2; 1.10; 2.3; 3.2; 4.3)

* Have the students conduct research to learn more about Harry Truman. Ask them to construct questions they would like to ask Truman about his life and the decisions he made. (1.1; 1.2; 1.5; 1.6)

* Have students log on to the web page for the Truman Library at www.whistlestop.org. The students can view documents, photographs, and cartoons about Truman and his presidency. There are also special activities and lessons for kids. (1.2; 1.4)

* Using the time line on page 322 as a guide, have the students determine how old Harry Truman was at the beginning of the Great Depression, at the American entrance into World War II, and at the end of the war in Korea. (1.4; 1.8)

* Have the children create a Wall of Famous Missourians. The students should develop criteria for choosing the individuals who should be included in this display. Have them use pictures, symbols, and words to identify each person they select for inclusion. (1.1; 1.2; 1.6; 2.1)

* Discuss with the students how Martin Luther King and Lucile Bluford worked to improve the democratic ideals of freedom, justice, and equality. Ask them to consider ways they can promote those same ideals. (1.2; 1.10; 2.3; 4.2; 4.3)

* Plan and develop a mural that depicts the story of Missouri. Divide the history of the state into several segments, such as the Native Americans, exploration and colonization, the westward movement, the Civil War, the early 1900s, and Missouri today. Separate the class into several groups and let each group illustrate one of the periods of history. (1.2; 2.1)

SUMMARY OF PRINCIPAL POINTS

This chapter deals with American involvement in World War II and how the United States became a world power. The roles Missourians played in fighting the wars, working in factories and on farms, and collecting waste products for war materials are discussed. Harry Truman's leadership of the nation from wartime to peacetime forms an important part of this chapter. The Civil Rights movement and the efforts of women to secure equal rights are also discussed. Harry Truman, the only Missourian to be president, and Lucile Bluford, a journalist and Civil Rights leader, are both profiled as Famous Missourians. Governor Forest Donnell's official proclamation calling upon Missourians to save used grease as a part of efforts to win World War II is the primary source document for this chapter.

ANSWERS TO QUESTIONS AND EXERCISES IN THE TEXT

In Their Own Words

1. Answers may vary. Suggested: lard, cooking oil, bacon grease, and other meat fats.

2. Fats contain glycerine. Glycerine was used in the manufacture of munitions, paints, medicines, and many other products.

3. Answers will vary. Suggested: Many Americans, including school children and boy and girl scouts, took part in drives to collect used grease, newspapers, scrap metal, and other materials that could be recycled to support the war effort.

4. To make it an official document.

5. Answers will vary. Suggested: Discuss the benefits of recycling and how it helps preserve valuable resources and protect the environment. Ask them to identify the kinds of things that we recycle today.

Testing Yourself

1. Germany, Italy, and Japan.

2. England, France, and the Soviet Union (Russia). Later the United States joined the Allies.

3. General Omar N. Bradley, General Maxwell Taylor, and Captain Wendell Pruitt.

4. Harry S. Truman.

5. Many Missourians joined the armed forces; they raised extra food in home gardens and on farms; Missouri factories produced clothing, airplanes, guns, and other war machines; Missouri mines provided iron, lead, and zinc. Missourians bought war bonds; they collected old newspapers, scrap metal, used grease, and other waste products; and many women took over the jobs of workers who had joined the armed forces.

6. Korea and Vietnam.

7. They went to court to end segregation. They also organized protest movements and marches to call attention to unfair treatment.

8. The commission is a group of people who try to ensure that all Missourians are given equal treatment.

Things to Talk About

1. Answers will vary.

2. Answers will vary.

3. Answers will vary. Suggested: Have the students conduct research to discover some of the things that the United Nations does today. They send peacekeeping forces to stop violence in some countries; they also send doctors and health care workers and provide food and other supplies for very poor countries.

4. Answers will vary. Suggested: Because Dr. King was a national leader in the movement to win equal treatment for African Americans and because he stood for justice and freedom for all Americans.

Using a Time Line

1. Louisiana Purchase Exposition, Great Depression Begins, United States Enters World War II, War in Vietnam Ends, Dr. Martin Luther King Leads a Civil Rights March on Washington, D.C.

2. Yes, he would have been about twenty years old when the fair was held, and he lived in Missouri.

CHAPTER 16

GOVERNMENT IN MISSOURI

What All Students Should Know

The Guiding Questions listed below are correlated with the text, and intended to assist teachers and curriculum designers with the development of unit and lesson plans. The applicable Show-Me Knowledge Standards for Social Studies are referenced in parentheses at the end of each question. A listing of those standards can be found on page 5 of this Guide.

1. Why do groups have rules? Why do societies have laws and governments? (SS3; SS6)

2. What are governments and what do they do? (SS1; SS3)

3. Why is it important to limit the powers of government? (SS1)

4. What are some of the purposes and ideals of government in the United States? (SS1; SS3)

5. How are different governments organized? How is government in the United States organized? (SS1; SS3)

6. How do governments affect people's lives? (SS3; SS6)

7. How do officials make, apply, and enforce rules and laws? How do they get the authority to do so? (SS1; SS3)

8. What services do governments provide? How do those services satisfy human wants? (SS3; SS4; SS7)

9. What resources do governments need to provide services? How do they obtain and pay for those services? (SS4; SS7)

10. What are some symbols associated with the United States and its government? What are some symbols associated with Missouri and its government? (SS1; SS6)

What All Students Should Be Able to Do

1.1. Develop questions and ideas to initiate and refine research.

1.2. Conduct research to answer questions and evaluate information and ideas.

1.3. Design and conduct field and laboratory investigations to study nature and society.

1.4. Use technological tools and other resources to locate, select, and organize information.

1.5. Comprehend and evaluate written, visual, and oral presentations and works.

1.6. Discover and evaluate patterns and relationships in information.

1.7. Evaluate the accuracy of information and ideas and the reliability of their sources.

1.8. Organize data, information, and ideas into useful forms for analysis or presentation.

1.9. Identify, analyze, and compare the institutions, traditions, and art forms of past and present societies.

1.10. Apply acquired information, ideas, and skills to different contexts.

2.1. Plan and make written, oral, and visual presentations for a variety of purposes and audiences.

2.2. Review and revise communications to improve accuracy and clarity.

2.3. Exchange information, questions, and ideas while recognizing the perspectives of others.

2.4. Present perceptions and ideas regarding works of the arts, humanities, and sciences.

2.5. Perform or produce works in the fine and practical arts.

2.7. Use technological tools to exchange information and ideas.

3.1. Identify problems and define their scope and elements.

3.2. Develop and apply strategies based on ways others have prevented or solved problems.

3.3. Develop and apply strategies based on one's own experiences in preventing or solving problems.

3.4. Evaluate the processes used in recognizing and solving problems.

3.5. Reason inductively from a set of specific facts and deductively from general premises.

3.6. Examine problems and proposed solutions from multiple perspectives.

3.7. Evaluate the extent to which a strategy addresses the problem.

3.8. Assess costs, benefits, and other consequences of proposed solutions.

4.1. Explain reasoning and identify information used to support decisions.

4.2. Understand and apply the rights and responsibilities of citizenship in Missouri and in the United States.

4.3. Analyze the duties and responsibilities of individuals in societies.

4.4. Recognize and practice honesty and integrity in academic work.

4.5. Develop, monitor, and revise plans of action to meet deadlines and accomplish those tasks.

Sample Learning Activities

The applicable Show-Me Performance Standards are referenced in parentheses.

* Have the students make up some rules for the classroom and compare classroom rules to those of home. Then have the students draw conclusions about why we need rules. (1.10; 4.3; 4.7)

* Invite officers from the police or fire department to visit the class and explain what they do. Ask them to respond to questions the students create. Use the occasion to discuss where police and fire officials get authority to exercise their powers and who makes the rules and laws they enforce. (1.1; 1.3; 1.10; 2.3)

* Have the students visit city hall or the county courthouse to find out what jobs of government are carried out in the rooms of the building. To conclude the activity, have students draw pictures of what they have seen or have them simulate a mock government based on their observations. (1.2; 1.3; 2.1)

* Arrange for a field trip to Jefferson City to visit the State Capitol and find out what jobs of government are carried out by the state government. If possible, arrange for students to meet with their state senator or representative and ask them to tell about their jobs. (1.2; 1.3; 2.3)

* Create a chart showing the relationship between national, state, and local (county and city) government. On the chart indicate some of the services that each provides. (1.8)

* Talk about who pays the people who work in the government. Talk about who supplies the money to build and operate bridges, roads, schools, and other public improvements and services.

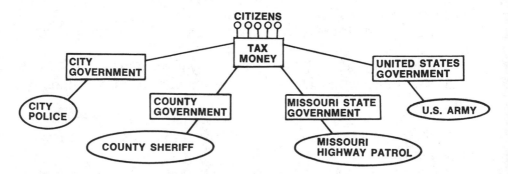

Draw this chart on a chalkboard or whiteboard to illustrate how taxes make it possible to provide those services. (1.2; 1.6; 1.8; 1.10; 4.2; 4.3)

* Set up a dramatization about a person who tries to buy a twenty-five-cent item with a quarter, only to find he or she also needs to pay a sales tax. Discuss what "plus tax" means and investigate what governments do with taxes. (1.10; 2.5; 4.2; 4.3)

* Make a pie chart to show where state tax monies go. (1.8)

* Stage an election in the class. It would be helpful if this were done during a national, state, or local election campaign. (1.10)

* Ask class members to bring current newspaper clippings describing recent activities of the current governor or some other public official. (1.2; 1.4)

* Ask the students to identify symbols associated with the United States. Review with them Missouri's state symbols found in the appendix of the textbook. Have the students draw pictures of these symbols. (2.5)

* Have the students log on to the State of Missouri Kids Page on the internet: www.gov.state.mo.us/kids/. The interactive site provides many activities for students. One of the things that they can do on the Kids Page is send the governor an email message. (1.4; 2.7)

SUMMARY OF PRINCIPAL POINTS

This chapter stresses the need for laws in an orderly society and discusses the role of government in making and enforcing those laws and in providing certain kinds of services. Democracy in the United States is explained, as are the different roles of the national government and the fifty state governments. There are brief descriptions of the organization of the national government and of local and state government in Missouri. How governments get the money necessary to carry out their functions is explained. The responsibilities of being a good citizen are also examined.

ANSWERS TO QUESTIONS AND EXERCISES IN THE TEXT

Testing Yourself

1. People need rules to prevent conflicts and to provide for the safety, welfare, and rights of everyone. Governments can also provide many services for the people.

2. Answers will vary. Suggested possibilities: traffic laws regulating speeding, reckless driving, failure to stop at a stop sign or traffic signal, etc.; criminal laws regulating murder, robbery, kidnapping, arson, etc.; environmental laws regulating waste disposal, air and water pollution, etc.; conservation laws regulating hunting, fishing, etc.; professional licensing laws regulating physicians, nurses, lawyers, teachers, and other professionals.

3. Legislative, executive, and judicial.

4. The national government maintains the army, the navy, the marines, and the air force; it make treaties with other countries; it prints our paper money and makes our coins; it maintains Social Security and Medicare to help take care of older Americans, and it operates national parks.

5. Each state government operates schools, builds roads and bridges, acts to protect lives and property, and also helps take care of people with special needs and problems.

6. City and county governments hire police officers and fire fighters to protect the people and their property. They build and take care of streets, roads, bridges, sewers, parks, and recreation centers, and some operate hospitals or animal shelters.

7. Sales tax, income tax, property tax, gasoline tax, and cigarette tax.

Choosing the Right Words
1. fifty.
2. general assembly.
3. governor.
4. jury.
5. a sales.
6. city council.

Things to Find out
Answers will vary.

Things to Do
1. Suggested: operates public elementary and secondary schools; operates public colleges and universities; hires law enforcement and fire protection officials to protect the people and their property; builds and takes care of streets, roads, and bridges; constructs and takes care of sewers; builds and maintains parks and helps preserve historic places; operates hospitals and provides health care services; operates public libraries; provides assistance for handicapped and needy people; protects the environment from pollution; encourages tourism and economic development in the state; and operates courts to settle disputes and punish people who break the law.

Things to Talk About
1. Answers will vary.
2. By holding elections. Groups that are formed to help get candidates elected to public office.

CHAPTER 17

MISSOURI AT THE START OF THE TWENTY-FIRST CENTURY

What All Students Should Know

The Guiding Questions listed below are correlated with the text and intended to assist teachers and curriculum designers with the development of unit and lesson plans. The applicable Show-Me Knowledge Standards for Social Studies are referenced in parentheses at the end of each question. A listing of those standards can be found on page 5 of this Guide.

1. What new technologies are changing the way people live in the twenty-first century? How have computers changed the way we do things? (SS2; SS6; SS7)

2. Why have recreation and tourism become so important to Missouri? (SS4; SS5)

3. Why should Missourians be concerned about protecting their environment? What are some of the principal threats to the environment? What steps have been taken to deal with those threats? (SS4; SS5; SCI8)

4. What new discoveries have been made as a result of space travel? (SS2)

What All Students Should Be Able to Do

1.1. Develop questions and ideas to initiate and refine research.

1.2. Conduct research to answer questions and evaluate information and ideas.

1.3. Design and conduct field and laboratory investigations to study nature and society.

1.4. Use technological tools and other resources to locate, select, and organize information.

1.5. Comprehend and evaluate written, visual, and oral presentations and works.

1.6. Discover and evaluate patterns and relationships in information.

1.7. Evaluate the accuracy of information and ideas and the reliability of their sources.

1.8. Organize data, information, and ideas into useful forms for analysis or presentation.

1.9. Identify, analyze, and compare the institutions, traditions, and art forms of past and present societies.

1.10. Apply acquired information, ideas, and skills to different contexts.

2.1. Plan and make written, oral, and visual presentations for a variety of purposes and audiences.

2.2. Review and revise communications to improve accuracy and clarity.

2.3. Exchange information, questions, and ideas while recognizing the perspectives of others.

2.4. Present perceptions and ideas regarding works of the arts, humanities, and sciences.

2.5. Perform or produce works in the fine and practical arts.

2.7. Use technological tools to exchange information and ideas.

3.1. Identify problems and define their scope and elements.

3.2. Develop and apply strategies based on ways others have prevented or solved problems.

3.3. Develop and apply strategies based on one's own experiences in preventing or solving problems.

3.4. Evaluate the processes used in recognizing and solving problems.

3.5. Reason inductively from a set of specific facts and deductively from general premises.

3.6. Examine problems and proposed solutions from multiple perspectives.

3.7. Evaluate the extent to which a strategy addresses the problem.

3.8. Assess costs, benefits, and other consequences of proposed solutions.

4.1. Explain reasoning and identify information used to support decisions.

4.2. Understand and apply the rights and responsibilities of citizenship in Missouri and in the United States.

4.3. Analyze the duties and responsibilities of individuals in societies.

4.4. Recognize and practice honesty and integrity in academic work.

4.5. Develop, monitor, and revise plans of action to meet deadlines and accomplish those tasks.

Sample Learning Activities

The applicable Show-Me Performance Standards are referenced in parentheses.

* Use the Think/Pair/Share cooperative learning structure to have students identify as many different uses of computers as they can. Ask them to give examples of how computers have changed the way Missourians live. Invite them to speculate about future changes that computers might make possible. (1.2; 2.3; 3.5)

* Have the students compile lists of Missouri's greatest attractions for visitors and tourists. Assign each regional committee created for chap-

ter 2 to develop a list of these attractions in their region. Review those lists and then have the class select Missouri's top ten attractions with a vote. When they have made their choices, have them prepare a tourist brochure with pictures and words that feature those attractions. (1.2; 1.4; 1.8; 2.1; 2.5)

* Have the students conduct research to identify any special environmental problems in Missouri. Discuss what responsibilities citizens have for protecting the environment. Consider what actions the students could take to help save the environment. (1.2; 1.10; 3.1; 3.2; 4.2; 4.3)

* Have the students log on to the NASA Kids Page at www.-nasa.gov/kids.html. There are many learning activities that will interest them. (1.4)

* Invite students to speculate about forms of transportation Missourians will use one hundred years from now. Ask them to write a paragraph about "Travel in the Year 2101." (2.3; 2.4)

* Discuss with the students what they think would most surprise and astonish someone who lived in French Missouri 250 years ago if she or he visited Missouri today. Have them write a letter describing what they might say. (1.9; 2.1)

* Have the students prepare a mural titled "Missouri: Then and Now" showing parallel views of early and modern Missouri. (1.9; 2.5)

* Ask students to consider what kinds of jobs they might like to have when they finish school. Have them conduct research to see what knowledge and skills would be required to obtain such a job. (1.2; 4.8)

SUMMARY OF PRINCIPAL POINTS

This chapter deals with changes in Missouri since World War II and shows how those changes have contributed to various aspects of Missouri society today. Topics discussed include the changing faces of Missourians, the computer age, farming, manufacturing, changes in merchandising and retailing, tourism and recreation, recreation and tourism, professional sports, protecting Missouri's environment, and transportation. Three astronauts, Tom Akers, Linda Godwin, and Janet Kavandi, are featured as Famous Missourians.

ANSWERS TO QUESTIONS AND EXERCISES IN THE TEXT

Things to Talk About

1. Computers have many different uses including manufacturing, record keeping, word processing, publishing, graphic design, finance and banking, communication, medical treatments, education, entertainment, and recreation. In the age of computer technologies and information services, workers need the skills to operate and maintain the different types of computers that are a part of daily life.

Computers have speeded up the process of handling, storing, and retrieving vast amounts of information.

2. Answers will vary.

3. Answers will vary.

4. Answers will vary. Suggested: Because of the rapid changes in the workplace, workers will probably hold several different jobs in one lifetime. People increasingly need a good education to make them ready for those changes.

Testing Yourself

1. Answers will vary. Suggested: They sort, store, and make large amounts of information available quickly and easily; they allow users to communicate with people all around the world instantly; they are used in homes, businesses, farms, factories, schools, and offices to keep records and to operate machines of all kinds, and they make it possible for people to make telephone calls, get money from a cash machine, and check out at a supermarket.

2. The Internet allows computer users to get all kinds of information from all over the world immediately.

3. Corn, wheat, cotton, grain sorghum, soybeans, rice, fruit and berries, cattle, poultry, hogs.

4. Modern machinery, chemicals, and fertilizers, and new scientific farming techniques have all made it possible to increase production.

5. Automobiles, airplanes and space vehicles, chemicals, food products, military weapons, computers and electronic equipment, clothing, shoes, soaps and detergents, paints, clay products, glass products, medical instruments, fabricated metal products, furniture, and household fixtures.

6. Its many recreational and historic attractions; its beautiful rivers, lakes, and scenic countryside; its caves; its professional sports teams, performing arts groups, libraries, museums, theaters, and theme parks.

7. They operate and maintain modern airports in many parts of the state. Missouri factories have produced airplanes and spacecraft, and many Missourians work in the airline industry; three Missourians have made space flights for NASA.

CHAPTER 18

FINE ARTS IN MISSOURI

What All Students Should Know

The Guiding Questions listed below are correlated with the text and are intended to assist teachers and curriculum designers with the development of unit and lesson plans. The applicable Show-Me Knowledge

Standards for Social Studies are referenced in parentheses at the end of each question. A listing of those standards can be found on page 5 of this Guide.

1. What qualities do you think make a good book or poem? What are your favorite kinds of books and poems? Who do you consider to have been some of the best writers from Missouri? Why? (SS6; FA2; FA5; CA2)

2. Who is your favorite Missouri artist? Why? (SS6; FA5)

3. What famous Missouri artists sometimes painted Missouri scenes? (FA5)

4. Why are different forms of music such as blues, jazz, and ragtime often associated with Missouri? Who were some famous African American musicians with ties to Missouri? (SS2; SS6; FA5)

What All Students Should Be Able to Do

1.1. Develop questions and ideas to initiate and refine research.

1.2. Conduct research to answer questions and evaluate information and ideas.

1.3. Design and conduct field and laboratory investigations to study nature and society.

1.4. Use technological tools and other resources to locate, select, and organize information.

1.5. Comprehend and evaluate written, visual, and oral presentations and works.

1.6. Discover and evaluate patterns and relationships in information.

1.7. Evaluate the accuracy of information and ideas and the reliability of their sources.

1.8. Organize data, information, and ideas into useful forms for analysis or presentation.

1.9. Identify, analyze, and compare the institutions, traditions, and art forms of past and present societies.

1.10. Apply acquired information, ideas, and skills to different contexts.

2.1. Plan and make written, oral, and visual presentations for a variety of purposes and audiences.

2.2. Review and revise communications to improve accuracy and clarity.

2.3. Exchange information, questions, and ideas while recognizing the perspectives of others.

2.4. Present perceptions and ideas regarding works of the arts, humanities, and sciences.

2.5. Perform or produce works in the fine and practical arts.

2.7. Use technological tools to exchange information and ideas.

3.1. Identify problems and define their scope and elements.

3.2. Develop and apply strategies based on ways others have prevented or solved problems.

3.3. Develop and apply strategies based on one's own experiences in preventing or solving problems.

3.4. Evaluate the processes used in recognizing and solving problems.

3.5. Reason inductively from a set of specific facts and deductively from general premises.

3.6. Examine problems and proposed solutions from multiple perspectives.

3.7. Evaluate the extent to which a strategy addresses the problem.

3.8. Assess costs, benefits, and other consequences of proposed solutions.

4.1. Explain reasoning and identify information used to support decisions.

4.2. Understand and apply the rights and responsibilities of citizenship in Missouri and in the United States.

4.3. Analyze the duties and responsibilities of individuals in societies.

4.4. Recognize and practice honesty and integrity in academic work.

4.5. Develop, monitor, and revise plans of action to meet deadlines and accomplish those tasks.

Sample Learning Activities

The applicable Show-Me Process Standards are referenced in parentheses.

* Read a passage from one of Mark Twain's books to your class. Discuss with the students the passages that you read. Invite them to discuss why they believe that Mark Twain was a great writer. Discuss some of Twain's best-known books. Ask if any of the students have read any of them. Ask them to construct a list of questions that they would like to ask Mark Twain about his life and writing. (1.1; 1.5; 1.9; 2.1; 2.4)

* Have the students conduct research to learn more about Langston Hughes. Read the two poems by Hughes that are in the text. Ask students to tell what they think the poems mean. Ask them to tell why they think his poems are so popular. Suggest that they read other poems by Hughes. Assign them to write a paragraph about Langston Hughes. (1.2; 1.5; 2.1; 2.4)

* Assign the students to read at least one book by a Missouri author. Have them write a short book report about the book. (1.5; 2.1; 2.4)

* View with the students "Changing Places," video no. 12 in the Finding Missouri series. Before watching it, invite the students to generate questions about Laura Ingalls Wilder that interest them. Following

the presentation of the video, allow student responses and questions to shape a general discussion about Wilder and her writing. (1.1; 1.2; 1.4; 1.5; 2.3)

* Ask the students to discuss what they think is required to write a book. Discuss how authors get their ideas for things to write about. What do they think would be the most difficult part of writing a book? (2.3; 2.4)

* Have the students identify their favorite Missouri author, artist, or musician and make a poster showing different things about their life and their work. (1.5; 2.1)

* Play short recordings of music composed or performed by some of Missouri's famous African American musicians. Discuss the importance of African American contributions to American music. (2.4)

* Divide the class into groups and assign each group to do research about a Missouri artist. Have them locate pictures showing their art in books, art catalogues, or on the internet. Ask them to prepare a presentation for the class about their artist. (1.2; 1.5; 2.1; 2.4)

SUMMARY OF PRINCIPAL POINTS

This chapter identifies some of Missouri's outstanding authors, artists, and musicians, and it stresses the use of Missouri subjects in the arts. As in other areas, Missourians have demonstrated great diversity in all fields of the fine and performing arts. Two poems written by Langston Hughes are included. Laura Ingalls Wilder is the featured Famous Missourian.

ANSWERS TO QUESTIONS AND EXERCISES IN THE TEXT

In Their Own Words
1. Answers will vary. Suggested: African Americans should be proud of their heritage.
2. Answers will vary. Suggested: Without dreams life would have little meaning.
3. Answers will vary.

Testing Yourself
1. Books, short stories, travel stories, "tall tales," poems.
2. Samuel Clemens (Mark Twain), Langston Hughes, Laura Ingalls Wilder, Eugene Field.
3. George Caleb Bingham, George Catlin, John James Audubon, Thomas Hart Benton, Walt Disney.
4. W. C. Handy, Scott Joplin, Charlie "Bird" Parker, William "Count" Basie.
5. A pen name is used by an author when he or she does not want readers to know his or her real name.
6. Walt Disney.

Matching Partners
1-f; 2-h; 3-i; 4-b; 5-a; 6-c; 7-j; 8-e; 9-d; 10-g

Things to Talk About
1. History is the story of things that actually happened, and fiction is a story that the author made up.

2. Answers will vary.

3. Answers will vary.

4. Answers will vary.

5. Answers will vary.

6. Answers will vary.

SELECTED BIBLIOGRAPHY

Burnett, Robyn K., and Ken Luebbering, *German Settlement in Missouri: New Land, Old Ways.* Columbia: University of Missouri Press, 1996.

Chapman, Carl H., and Eleanor F. Chapman. *Indians and Archaeology of Missouri.* Rev. ed. Columbia: University of Missouri Press, 1983.

Christensen, Lawrence O., William E. Foley, Gary R. Kremer, and Kenneth H. Winn, eds. *Dictionary of Missouri Biography.* Columbia: University of Missouri Press, 1999.

Christensen, Lawrence O., and Gary R. Kremer. *A History of Missouri: Volume IV, 1875-1919.* Columbia: University of Missouri Press, 1997.

Dains, Mary K., and Sue Sadler, eds. *Show Me Missouri Women.* 2 vols. Kirksville, Mo.: Thomas Jefferson University Press, 1989, 1993.

Dyer, Robert L. *Jesse James and the Civil War in Missouri.* Columbia: University of Missouri Press, 1994.

Flader, Susan, ed. *Exploring Missouri's Legacy: State Parks and Historic Sites.* Columbia: University of Missouri Press, 1992.

Foley, William E. *A History of Missouri: Volume I, 1673-1820.* Columbia: University of Missouri Press, paperback edition, 1999.

————. *Genesis of Missouri: From Wilderness Outpost to Statehood.* Columbia: University of Missouri Press, 1989.

Greene, Lorenzo J., Gary R. Kremer, and Antonio F. Holland. *Missouri's Black Heritage.* Rev. ed. Columbia: University of Missouri Press, 1993.

Humphrey, Loren. *Quinine and Quarantine: Missouri Medicine through the Years.* Columbia: University of Missouri Press, 2000.

Kirkendall, Richard S. *A History of Missouri: Volume V, 1919-1953.* Columbia: University of Missouri Press, 1986.

McCandless, Perry. *A History of Missouri: Volume II, 1820-1860.* Columbia: University of Missouri Press, paperback edition, 2000.

McMillan, Margot Ford. *Paris, Tightwad, and Peculiar: Missouri Place Names.* Columbia: University of Missouri Press, 1994.

March David D. *The History of Missouri.* 4 vols. New York: Lewis Historical Publishing Co., 1967.

Matson, Madeline. *Food in Missouri: A Cultural Stew.* Columbia: University of Missouri Press, 1994.

Parrish, William E. *A History of Missouri: Volume III, 1860-1875.* Columbia: University of Missouri Press, paperback edition, 2001.

Parrish, William E., Charles T. Jones, Jr. and Lawrence O. Christensen. *Missouri: Heart of the Nation.* Arlington Heights, Ill.: Harlan Davidson, 1992.

Priddy, Bob. *Across Our Wide Missouri.* 2 vols. Independence, Mo.: Independence Press, 1982-1984.

Rogers, Ann. *Lewis and Clark in Missouri.* Rev. ed. St. Louis: Meredco, 1993.

Shoemaker, Floyd C. *Missouri and Missourians.* 4 vols. Chicago: Lewis Publishing
    Co., 1943.